WHEN WOMEN RUN THE FIRM

How to successfully launch and manage your law practice with confidence

Demetria L. Graves,
**Attorney and Certified Family Law Specialist
Certified by the California State Bar Board of Legal Specialization**

When Women Run the Firm © 2021 Demetria L. Graves

All rights reserved. No part of this publication may be reproduced, distributed or transmitted in any form or by any means, including photocopying, recording, or other electronic or mechanical methods, without the prior written permission of the publisher, except in the case of brief quotations embodied in critical reviews and certain other noncommercial uses permitted by copyright law.

Although the author and publisher have made every effort to ensure that the information in this book was correct at press time, the author and publisher do not assume and hereby disclaim any liability to any party for any loss, damage, or disruption caused by errors or omissions, whether such errors or omissions result from negligence, accident, or any other cause.

Adherence to all applicable laws and regulations, including international, federal, state and local governing professional licensing, business practices, advertising, and all other aspects of doing business in the US, Canada or any other jurisdiction is the sole responsibility of the reader and consumer.

Neither the author nor the publisher assumes any responsibility or liability whatsoever on behalf of the consumer or reader of this material. Any perceived slight of any individual or organization is purely unintentional.

The resources in this book are provided for informational purposes only and should not be used to replace the specialized training and professional judgment of a health care or mental health care professional.

Neither the author nor the publisher can be held responsible for the use of the information provided within this book. Please always consult a trained professional before making any decision regarding treatment of yourself or others.

For more information, email: demetria.gravesesq@gmail.com

ISBN: 978-1-7371415-7-0 (paperback)

ISBN: 978-1-7371415-0-1 (ebook)

Aiden. Mom. Dad. Det.

Thank you. I love you.

None of this is possible without you.

GET YOUR FREE GIFT!

This action guide is best used in conjunction with *When Women Run the Firm: How to successfully launch and manage your law practice with confidence.*

If you don't have a copy, then today is your lucky day! You can grab your copy for FREE here: https://firmactionguide.ck.page/a05c31a9fd

CONTENTS

Introduction *1*

PILLAR 1 – What Is Your "Why"? 13

PILLAR 2 – Commit 17

PILLAR 3 – The Business of Running Your Law Firm 19

PILLAR 4 – Law Firm Management 35

PILLAR 5 – Marketing 69

PILLAR 6 – Client Management 71

PILLAR 7 – The Court Experience 77

PILLAR 8 – The Infamous "Work/Life Balance" 83

PILLAR 9 – If I Knew Then What I Know Now 87

PILLAR 10 – It Takes a Village 93

The Completed Outline! Here it is... 143

Introduction

On July 5, 2015, I opened the doors to the Law Offices of Demetria L. Graves. Twenty-five years old, six months out of law school, jobless, and no business ownership experience. But I took the leap anyway. Determined. Fearless. Unaware. This book is a culmination of everything I experienced, learned, and wish I knew when I started.

What I now know for sure is that law firm ownership is challenging for any attorney, and the task is even more challenging for female attorneys as we will discuss. According to the American Bar Association, women make up only 36% of the profession, and an even smaller percentage are women of color: 5% of lawyers are African American, 5% Hispanic, and 3% Asian (but these numbers include both women and men of color).

I could write an entire book on my experience as a minority woman practicing law and starting my own practice at just 25 years old. On this journey, I have met great attorneys who took the time to mentor and support me, and as you can imagine, I experienced not so great attorneys who attempted to take advantage of me. But every single experience taught me about not only the Family Law experience, but also who I wanted to be as a lawyer and as a person.

As I would like to believe, we are making great strides to close the gender inequality gap, but as shown by the numbers above, we still have a long way to go. In addition to the dismal numbers, female attorneys (in most families) still shoulder the responsibility of child rearing, sometimes caring for aging parents, serving as helpmates to spouses/partners, and a list of other responsibilities.

With so much responsibility, it is no surprise that some female attorneys may be extremely hesitant to take the leap of faith and open their own law practice. Even if there is interest in law firm ownership, many do not know HOW to take the leap and continue to tend to their many other responsibilities. The questions I hear most are: "What do I do?" and "Where will I get clients?" And the ultimate question is: "Do I have what it takes to do this?" I am here to tell you that, despite your fears, it is possible.

Based on my 15 years of law firm ownership, I have provided the ins and outs of law firm ownership and everything in between. When I initially started my practice, I had so many questions and few answers, and I made A LOT of mistakes. I did not have most of the information that I have provided here. Most law schools do not teach us how to be entrepreneurs, how to run businesses, and how to manage a law practice, which are all necessary skills for running your own practice. What I do remember from law school is the push to earn great grades, get to the top 20% (at least) of

INTRODUCTION

your class, and go work for a great firm and make six figures while billing insane monthly hours. This is a great plan if that's what you want to do.

Well, what about the remaining 80% of most law school graduates who do not land fancy, big-time law firm positions? What about the lawyers who do not want to be slaves to billable hours and become strangers to their families? What about the women who want to be present for their children but still pursue a career? Even after law school and transitioning into firm practice, it would be nice to have an introduction to law firm management in order to allow one the option to consider whether law firm ownership is a possibility either after law school or some time down the line.

Like most of you, I did not have any formal business training, I was not at the top of my class, and I simply did not want to work insane hours and stay in an office buried under paperwork all day. Without the comfort of a real plan or experience, I opened my practice, and by way of experience, a lot of trial and error, learning from others, and simply wanting to equip my fellow sisters in the law, I created this resource.

So, Who Is This Book For?

Simple. This is for you if you are a woman considering law firm ownership. This is for you if you are terrified to make the leap from law firm practice to law firm ownership because you simply do not know how to do it. This is for you if you have considered the possibility for months but have not taken the next step. This is for you if you have started to reach out to other successful law firm business owners, but you are paralyzed by fear. This is for you if you constantly think about the possibility, but quickly dismiss the idea because you need your current salary. This is for you if you are tired of constantly choosing between writing that last memo before going home for the day or attending your kids' soccer/basketball/football/cheer event.

This is also for you if you have recently opened your practice and simply need guidance. This is for you if you just feel alone and ostracized because you are new to the solo practice world, and you are treated "differently" from the "big boys."

WHO IS DEMETRIA L. GRAVES?

Wow, this all sounds amazing, right? But who am I, and why should you even care or listen to what I have to say? Well, we know women are always right, right? LOL. Kidding, kind of. Okay. Let me tell you my story.

I am Demetria L. Graves, and I am a "Certified" Family Law specialist, which is just a fancy way to say I took an additional test (similar to a mini bar exam, but with a Family Law focus) to become recognized as a specialist in my practice area, Family Law, by submitting an application to the state bar of California, similar to the moral character application we submit to become attorneys. Over the years I have collected my share of accolades, including National Bar Association, Top 40 Under 40 Attorney (2018), Southern California Super Lawyer since 2016, Rising Star early in my career, listed among the Los Angeles Business Journal's 2021 Most Influential Minorities: Attorneys List, and the

INTRODUCTION

Los Angeles Business Journal's 2020 "Thriving in their 40's list." I serve on many boards and had the opportunity to be the President of Black Women Lawyers Association of Los Angeles. I also host a podcast, Legally Uncensored, which is perfect for those navigating the legal system or for those who are just interested in celebrity drama, as I break down celebrity legal headlines and discuss how listeners can best handle these types of legal challenges should they arise in their own lives.

After graduating from UC Berkeley (Go Bears!), I graduated from Loyola Law School, Los Angeles in 2004, passed the bar in November 2004, and started working for a small Family Law firm in December 2004.

I hated it. I stayed for approximately six months and remember distinctly thinking that if my next experience was anything like "this," I would leave the practice of law. What is "this" you ask? I was thrown into the world of Family Law (without really knowing what Family Law was at the time) with no training and seated in a cubicle with an unfriendly office staff. It was brutal for me. I hated to ask questions, and the experience was not what I envisioned when I fantasized about my experience in law school. I was thinking more Ally McBeal (I'm sure some of you do not know who Ally McBeal is), you know, something elaborate. It is plausible that I set my sights too high, but in any event, the law firm was not a good fit. I knew I should have left when I often cried on my way to work, but I felt like I needed the money (which was very little by the way). But there was a silver lining and ultimately the foundation for starting my own law practice. I did not enjoy the firm, but I did enjoy

Family Law, and although I had received very little training at the firm, I did gain useful experience.

By the time I left six months later, the job had become unbearable, and I was very discouraged and miserable. Depressed, because this was just not how I envisioned my law experience starting out, I called my mentor at the time to ask if she knew of any employment possibilities in Family Law. While I was still feeling sorry for myself and reconsidering my entire life, she asked me, "Why not open your own law practice?" Blindsided by the question, I thought, What? Me? Six months after passing the bar exam? Bombing my first firm experience? Right out of law school, first generation lawyer and business owner, little money in reserves, limited experience. No. Absolutely not.

I thought about every reason why I was not able to start my own firm, and ultimately, I was afraid. I did not believe I could own anything other than my six-year-old car at the time. Totally dismissing the thought, I started looking for opportunities in Family Law firms (no, my mentor never suggested any opportunities outside of me opening my own practice). I went on countless interviews, and two months later, I was still jobless.

I continued to communicate with my mentor during this time, and she continued to encourage me to at least consider law firm ownership. Now that I had been jobless for two months, the process of applying for jobs, going on countless interviews, and waiting on calls that I would never receive started to wear on me. I begin to tell myself that if "my firm" (the mere thought made me nervous) did not work out, I could always go back to looking for a job or I could continue

INTRODUCTION

to look for work as I took clients on a temporary basis. Believing I would only do this temporarily until I found work, I decided to do it.

Knowing for sure that I was crazy, I told my grandparents and my mother. All were skeptical of my decision, but they supported me, nonetheless. Shocked that they did not object too much, I then told a few friends, and they too were skeptical but still supported me, or at least they acted as though they did. LOL.

Once I made the decision to actually try out "my firm" (temporarily of course) and received the approval of those close to me (because, you know, at 25, you must have approval), in May of 2005, I started to arrange what I thought was important—I created letterhead with a nice logo and purchased a little file cabinet. Once organized, I picked a day to open my doors: July 5, 2005 (no real importance, just the day after the 4th of July). In my mind I was ready to go, so with my templates, letterhead, and cell phone, I opened The Law Offices of Demetria L. Graves. Little did I know, I was far from prepared for what was ahead of me.

When I opened my firm, I did not have the security of a "blueprint," a detailed step-by-step guide of how to establish a sustainable practice, which I have done my best to provide in detail here. Over the years, I have learned so much in my own practice and have spoken to several female law firm owners who have also learned a lot about law firm and business ownership. I want to give you all the information I possibly can, so I created this resource for you so that you can avoid opening your law practice the hard way (yeah, don't do what I did).

I made a lot of mistakes, but now you have the benefit of learning everything that I now know without making all the mistakes I made. Everything I have provided here I wish I would have known when I opened my practice 15 years ago. You will also get to read the advice of my esteemed colleagues, and most importantly, you will have a workable plan when you complete the book. I share with you many of my mistakes and essentially hold your hand as you prepare to open your own law firm practice. Use this blueprint to tackle the fear and the uncertainty most feel (including me) when deciding to open a law practice.

I am also a single parent to the best son in the world, so I definitely understand the family/law firm balancing act! After I had him, the balancing act most mothers face, the career versus motherhood debate and struggle, began. I constantly felt guilty when I was not able to show up in my practice the way that I did prior to my son's birth, and I also felt guilty when I left him in the care of my mother or grandparents more than I wanted. The constant tug-of-war was and is still a challenge, but I find a way each and every day to make it work, which I will discuss.

WHAT WILL YOU LEARN?

Yes, law firm ownership is a lot of work. The beauty is that you are working for yourself, your firm, and your legacy. With that said, embrace the journey, and embrace that the journey is a marathon, not a sprint. Very few attorneys who start their own law practice reach instant success without years of hard work. I remember hearing "It may take 20 years to be an overnight sensation." My goal is to leave you

INTRODUCTION

with all the tools and advice to empower you to take the leap of faith, and the rest is up to you.

I talk to a lot of young women considering law firm ownership, and many believe or have a false sense that once you open your doors, the firm will thrive immediately. I am here to tell you, like I tell them, for 95%, or I would even say 99% of us, this is just false. It takes YEARS, in most cases, to be an overnight success or to be the go-to person in your area or one of the go-to professionals in your area.

After practicing for 15 years, I believe a successful law firm must be built on a strong foundation to ensure continued success. A strong law firm foundation is based on what I believe to be 10 important pillars. The first pillar is a continued belief in yourself and your ability to run/operate your own business. The self-doubt and fear may temporarily paralyze you, but believe me, it is possible. The second pillar is a firm commitment to yourself and to your business, so that you can revisit your commitment to yourself and your business when you experience troubled waters. The third pillar is understanding the business of law firm ownership. It is important to understand that you are running a business first and a law practice second. The fourth pillar is the nuts-and-bolts of law firm management (yes, this is different from business ownership). The fifth pillar covers marketing. If people do not know how to find you, it does not matter how great of a lawyer you are. The sixth pillar covers client management to ensure that you are providing excellent service. The seventh pillar outlines your first court experience in your own firm. The eighth pillar examines the myth of work/life balance and explains the importance of taking care of yourself and your family on this journey. The ninth pillar outlines all of the important lessons I have learned along the way that I wish I would have known when I started my practice. And the final pillar, the tenth pillar, "It Takes a Village," is an inside look from other female attorneys and their perspectives on law firm ownership. One pillar is not more important than another—all pillars work together for your long-term success.

WHAT WILL YOU LEARN IN EACH PILLAR?

Pillar 1: What is your "Why"? Pillar 1 examines your reasons for opening your law firm. Your "Why" will help sustain you when the troubles of law firm ownership try to weigh you down. This pillar also examines any obstacles and self-limiting beliefs you may feel. You know how we always hear that a house must be built on a strong foundation or it will crumble in the event of an earthquake, a flood, etc.? The same principle applies to law firm ownership. It must be built on a strong foundation, which first starts with you.

Pillar 2: How committed are you to yourself and to your business? In this pillar, we discuss the importance of committing to yourself and to your business. There will be times when you want to quit and go build someone else's dream in another law practice. When these times come, you will remind yourself of your commitment to yourself and your business, and you will happily remind yourself why you started in the first place.

INTRODUCTION

Pillar 3: Time to work. We explore the importance of understanding the business aspect of your law firm. Your law firm is a business first, and you want to ensure that you are covered legally, you create a corporation or other entity that best fits your business, and you are aware of all city, state, federal and State Bar requirements for law firm management. In Pillar 3, I break down eight business considerations for you to think about before opening the business.

Pillar 4: After we tackle the business of law firm management in Pillar 3, we then examine law firm management and tips to manage your law firm as effectively as possible. The fourth pillar examines 11 for your consideration for law firm management.

Pillar 5: I dedicated an entire pillar to marketing because essentially marketing is your business. We discuss why marketing is so important for the success of your business and tips that you can immediately implement to get your name out there.

Pillar 6: Now that we have conquered the business of running the firm and managing the law firm, we now have to manage the client! In Pillar 6, we tackle client management.

Pillar 7: The first time appearing in court can be extremely daunting. I walk you through the experience of court (at least from the Family Law perspective) and provide tips for easing the nervousness you may feel when you appear in court for the first time on your own.

Pillar 8: In this pillar, I focus on the infamous work/life balance. I challenge you to reframe how you prioritize everything that you have to do in your life, even when building a practice. The unfair notion that we can "balance" everything at one time is unfair and unreasonable.

Pillar 9: Boy! Would my life be so different if I knew then what I know now, but I most likely would not have written this book. In this pillar, I summarize some of my biggest lessons, essentially a cheat sheet for you to reference on your journey.

Pillar 10: This pillar will provide you with tips and experiences from other successful female business owners from all different practice areas and life experiences. I wanted to give you a different perspective so that you:

1. Know that you are not alone;

2. Understand that there is not one way to operate a law practice; and

3. Even if you try your practice and decide you want to do something different later, that is okay!

After each pillar, I have begun to draft your blueprint so that you have a working document with all the assignments and tasks when you complete the book. Please feel free to change what I have provided to create your masterpiece.

Now that you are aware of what to expect, let's do this!

PILLAR 1

What Is Your "Why"?

Your "Why" is the most important foundational block you need to be clear on before you proceed with the other aspects of opening your business.

When I opened my practice, my confidence was primarily fueled by my mentor's belief that I could handle my own law practice. During that time, I never considered the importance of really spending time with my "Why." In hindsight, now that I have been on this journey, I should have taken more time to really consider my "Why" and the true responsibility of law firm ownership. Why is this important? If your "Why" is strong, when the hard times come (and they do come), you will remind yourself why you started in the first place. Your "Why" should be something that really moves and motivates you to keep going in trying times. My reasons for opening my practice at the time were very superficial: I was frustrated by my legal experience, I needed to make money, and let us not forget about the $100,000 student loan debt that I owed. I figured that because I was ambitious and smart, I would "figure it out." I focused solely on the financial experience and not on the soul-connecting experience. Essentially, my firm was birthed from necessity, which left little room for planning and a deeper understanding of my upcoming responsibility.

Because I did not have a strong "Why" as my anchor, when troubled times presented themselves, I was rocked every which way by difficult clients and condescending opposing counsel. I took cases that I knew I should have refused and allowed "more experienced" attorneys to discourage me. Without a stern belief in your abilities (I don't care how new or "experienced" you are), you will lack both the foundation you need to do what you intuitively know is best and the courage to stand up for your abilities and what you know is right. Yes, you will have questions about your cases and the law, but do not second-guess your ability to do the work you know how to do and your intuition. Your intuition is your inner guide that knows how to lead you, despite your self-doubt and fears.

You will continually be tested, and when the time comes that you question why you even started this journey in the first place, your "Why" will encourage you to keep trying because you will remember why you started.

Each "Why" will vary. After practicing for 15 years, I can now tell you, I love the autonomy of law firm ownership. I make my own schedule: I block out the days I do not want to work, and I do not need a reason to do so. I attend most of my son's school activities, take him to school and pick him up, and serve as an active parent at his school and in his extra-curricular activities. I have the flexibility to select my staff and my clients. I decide where my office will be located or whether or not I even need an office. I also select what systems I want to use in the firm, create legal strategies that I believe will work best for each client, mentor other attorneys, and grow my firm in my own way. I like to treat others with respect and provide the best services as possible to clients. I create jobs, stimulate the economy, and will leave a legacy for my family and a place for my son to work if he so chooses. I do not have to bill insane hours to make a living, and I have a life outside my law practice. This is my "Why."

So, what is your "Why"? Your "Why" should reflect your anchor when the practice gets challenging. Do you want to have more time with your family? Kids? Do you want to create your own schedule? Do you want to travel more? Earn more money? Avoid the politics of big law firms? Only you know the answer. Your turn! What is your "Why"?

MY LAW FIRM BLUEPRINT

PILLAR 1

1. What is my "Why"?

What is stopping you?

I never dreamed of law firm ownership, and truthfully, the idea scared me. The early days were overwhelming. I did not know what to do or how to even get started. In addition to feeling overwhelmed, my own personal limiting beliefs flooded my thoughts. Some of my favorite limiting beliefs at the time were: You cannot do this; You are too young; No one will hire you right out of law school; You have no money; You do not know anyone in the industry; You are a minority; You are a woman; You are a minority woman. The list goes on.

I moved forward in fear, and eventually, the beliefs faded or I learned to feel the fear and do it anyway. As I continued the practice throughout the years, I was more grounded, and I was no longer afraid. It is okay to be fearful, nervous, and unsure, but I encourage you to address as many fears as possible before you get started and to be as confident as you can possibly be.

What are your fears? What are your limiting beliefs? What is truly stopping you from making the next step? If you made it through law school, graduated, passed the bar, and have some experience in your practice area, you have the foundation you need if this is truly something you want to do. You got this! Unlike me, you will now have a plan of action to assist you, eliminating some of the stress of not understanding the next steps.

Take a minute to journal: "What is stopping me? What are my own limiting beliefs that may also be hindering me from moving forward?" Write out everything you can possibly think of.

MY LAW FIRM BLUEPRINT

PILLAR 1

1. *What is my "Why"?*
2. *What are my fears?*
3. *What are my limiting beliefs?*

PILLAR 2

Commit

Like understanding your "Why" and your limiting beliefs, for long-term success, you have to be willing to make a commitment to yourself and your law firm journey (oh boy, the journey) and a commitment to your business. When I started, I assumed I would "figure 'it' out." Yes, I did figure things out, but the storms were sometimes massive, sometimes small, and always discouraging in the beginning. I was not ready for the challenges I faced, and because I did not make a solid commitment to myself and to my business, each challenge rocked me to my core. I would become so upset and discouraged that I would start looking for jobs because, you know, everyone else can do this better than me. When I really got frustrated, I looked to external "fixes" such as unsuccessful partnerships, failed courses, unused programs, and the list continues. During my journey, I also did not provide myself enough forgiveness, self-love, and support when times were challenging. You MUST be patient and give yourself space to learn and grow when you make mistakes and get discouraged.

The bottom line is that I was not committed enough to myself and the business, and I wanted outside forces to "fix" what only I was responsible for fixing. After my "aha" moment and, frankly, a good look in the mirror, I decided to write out a commitment contract to myself and the business. My commitment contract is as follows:

> *I, Demetria L. Graves, fully commit to myself and to my practice. As of today's date, I will stop seeking external validation for myself and my practice, and I am now fully committed to building my practice without overly depending on outside forces to do my work. I take complete responsibility for my business, and I am willing to do what I know it takes to be successful. I will no longer attempt to achieve success by playing small and believing other people/things can "save" me. It is now my intention to show up for myself and my practice to the best of my ability and to be as honest as I can with myself as I continue my business journey. I can do the work, I am willing to do the work, and I am committed to doing the work.*

Now, it's your turn. WRITE OUT your commitment contract to yourself. When times get tough—and they will get tough—read your contract to yourself and remind yourself why you started. You might even decide to revisit and update your plan every six months, every year, etc., but do not skip this step!

PILLAR 2

> *WRITE OUT my commitment contract to myself and my practice.*

PILLAR 3
The Business of Running Your Law Firm

After you have established your "Why" and made a strong commitment to yourself and your business, it is now time to do the heavy lifting. Before we tackle law firm management, please understand that you are first running a business. At all times, you will need to ensure that the business side of the firm is properly operating, in addition to managing your practice. Television glamorizes all the positives of running a business such as fancy clothes and big fancy cases, nice vacations, and dinner at the most expensive restaurants. What we often do not see are the "boring" necessities of what it looks like to run a business: the everyday hustle, and the blood, sweat, and tears of business ownership. Running a business is work, and certainly not for the faint of heart.

Like just about everything in this book, I learned the importance of managing the business aspect of the firm while on the job. For example, I jumped in and only focused on making money and finding cases, not on researching what was necessary to run the business, such as city licensing, city taxes, business taxes, business formation options, an assessment of my fixed personal and business expenses, etc. I guess I can say "I did not know, what I did not know," meaning that my business foundation was extremely weak. You will always have to work "on" your business just as much as you work "in" your selected practice area.

Luckily, I made it through those early years with minimal damage, but I do not want this for you. I want you to be as equipped and prepared as you can possibly be, and maybe even more prepared.

Extra Credit: Interview three attorneys in your practice area and ask about their experience of running a BUSINESS. What do they enjoy about running a business? What don't they enjoy? What advice can they share with you about running both a practice and a law firm? Is there anything they would do differently? Add your questions as well! Go for it. P.S.: Offer to pay for their time, coffee/lunch! Talking to those who have experienced this process will give you great insight.

PILLAR 3

Interview with Three Attorneys

1. Attorney 1:

2. Attorney 2:

3. Attorney 3:

PILLAR 3 – THE BUSINESS OF RUNNING YOUR LAW FIRM

YOU ARE RUNNING A BUSINESS.

The purpose of establishing and managing the business side of your practice is to ensure that both you and your business are protected. Each city/state provides different rules for operating your business, as does the State Bar in your state. You want to ensure that you are following city, county, and state laws; State Bar rules; and employment laws if you employ others. Also, you have the flexibility to identify systems designed to smoothly run your business, so you can get out there and practice law, market your practice, and be the best attorney you can possibly be.

What should you include in your law firm blueprint when considering the business aspect of your business?

What I have included is not an exhaustive list of EVERYTHING needed, and you may decide to add different important business aspects that are unique to your practice, but I have included what I feel is important.

1. OWNING THE BUSINESS NAME

When I opened my practice, I named my firm/business "The Law Offices of Demetria L. Graves." I put the name on everything. Letterhead. Business cards. Logo. Etc. Very cool to see my name everywhere, but I missed an especially important step—I did not check with the California Secretary of State to ensure that "The Law Offices of Demetria L. Graves" was available before I used my credit card to make sure it looked nice on my firm's materials. Luckily, when I was informed that I should probably check, the name was in fact available, and I was able to properly register my business name. Just like business formation and business taxes, name selection is extremely important. You want to ensure that your business name of choice is available before you start holding yourself out by a name that is not properly registered with your state. Your business name captures your current and future goals for your practice.

Consider your goals for your law firm. You may want to include associates later, such as "Graves and Associates." I mean, I'm not sure that I like "Graves and Associates" ... it sounds like death, but you understand. You may want to add a partner later, and the list continues. I would say, write out at least 2-5 names before making your final decision.

You are not obligated to select a name based on what you have observed other attorneys do. Take some time to think about it, and select what is best for you and what makes sense for your practice now and potentially down the line.

Homework: Write down 2-5 law firm names that you like. You can also go to the Secretary of State's website where you are located and identify whether the names you have selected are available. Discuss your selected name with your business formation professional for the correct way to "own" your selected name. Ask three trusted mentors/friends for feedback about the names you have selected.

LEGAL NAME

1. *What names are fitting for my law practice?*

    1) Name 1:

    2) Name 2:

3) Name 3:

4) Name 4:

5) Name 5:

2. *Are the names selected available?*

3. *What steps do I need to take to legally own my selected name?*

4. *What names do my trusted mentors/friends like best?*

2. BUSINESS FORMATION

When I finally considered the importance of running a business and understanding that business was more than waking up and chasing clients every day, I formed an "S Corp" because I "heard" that with an S Corporation, I was protected if someone attempted to sue me, and "all" I had to do was pay a fee of $835 per year to keep the protection. So basically, I formed the corporation without talking to a business formation lawyer, CPA, etc. to discuss all my options. I read about the "pass through" protection and business protection of an S Corp, and I simply assumed that I understood everything about an S Corp (NOT) without considering other formation options. The audacity. I completed the incorporation documents myself (failing several times before it was right). An S Corp included more than just the registration of the corporation, and believe me, the State of California reminded me of my responsibilities.

I strongly suggest that you understand the difference in formation entities before deciding if and how you will incorporate. In the beginning, you may decide to simply become a "Sole Proprietor" and "DBA" (Do Business As) under the name you select for your firm. There are varying ways to form your business, and each business will vary depending on your practice area and your personal and business needs. The business entities tend to provide some level of protection for you and your firm. The typical business entities include (please understand this may not be an inclusive list, and I am surely not the one to guide you in this regard, I just want you to be aware!):

1. Limited Liability Partnership (LLP)
2. Limited Liability Limited Partnership (LLLP)
3. Professional Corporation (PC)
4. Limited Liability Corporation (LLC)

The best business formation for your firm should give you the best possible tax protection and the least liability exposure. Make the time to discuss your business needs and your practice area with a professional who is versed in business formation to ensure that you select the corporation most fitting for your firm. Fully understand your needs, and then decide once you understand how each corporation works and what is best for you—not your friends, your old firm, or like me, what you "heard." Once you have selected the best formation for your firm, you also want to discuss and understand your ongoing duty after the corporation is formed.

PILLAR 3 - THE BUSINESS OF RUNNING YOUR LAW FIRM

BUSINESS FORMATION

Business professional I will meet:

1. Based on my meeting with the business professional, what corporation is best for my business?

2. Will I incorporate the business myself, or will I hire someone to do this step for me?

---

3. BUSINESS TAXES

I know that my CPA hated me during the first three years of my practice. I did not keep great records during the year, and then I complained that my tax preparer had to spend more time than normally necessary to accurately report my income and expenses. Yes, of course, I wanted to pay the least amount of money for the most work. Eventually, I learned to keep better records during the year to avoid the headache of getting the documents together for my taxes. With your business formation comes business taxes if you have selected any form of "corporation." Your choice of entity will heavily impact your business, any taxes you may owe for operating your business, and (in some cases) personal taxes.

With most corporations, you are required to do quarterly business reporting and, of course, yearly tax returns. This is all in addition to your personal tax return, and the exact forms will largely depend on your business entity. Unless you have a solid background in corporate tax, I do not recommend that you take on this task on your own. While some do, I just do not recommend it. I strongly suggest that you find an experienced CPA to assist you with filing your corporate tax returns. I also attempt to meet with my CPA at the six-month mark to ensure I am on track and to adjust anything I need to adjust.

In addition to federal and state taxes, most cities also require you to obtain a business license and to pay city taxes, which should also be included in your tax planning.

If you plan to hire employees (including yourself if you will be an employee of your firm), you will also need to know the full cost of hiring employees, including required taxes.

Ultimately, you will want to ensure that you cross all T's and dot all I's. Please do not skip your business formation and tax exposure step. A detailed discussion with a business formation attorney, CPA, or other professional in this area will go a long way.

BUSINESS TAXES

CPA professional I will meet:

1. Name 1:
2. Name 2:
3. Name 3:

After my meeting:

1. What are my tax obligations based on my corporation?
2. Do I need a business license?

PILLAR 3 – THE BUSINESS OF RUNNING YOUR LAW FIRM

3. *Am I required to pay city taxes?*

4. *What is my tax obligation if I hire employees?*

5. *How often should I meet with my CPA?*

4. CITY LICENSING AND FEES

In addition to State and Federal Taxes, most cities require business owners to obtain a city business license and pay fees to the city. Be sure to inquire if your city requires a business license and if there are fees you are responsible for each year.

CITY LICENSING FEES

1. *Does my city require a business license?*

2. *If so, what fees am I responsible for each year?*

5. MANAGING BUSINESS INCOME/EXPENSES

Organization is key. The more organized you are with managing your business income/expenses, the easier the tax process will be. In the beginning, I had no clue what I was doing. I was a total mess.

I eventually wanted to ensure that I minimized any penalties and know that my business was in order. I did not want to be the reason for a delay in my tax filings, and I just really wanted to manage my business better. After two years of doing it the hard way, I hired a part-time bookkeeper to track my business income and expenses and to make sure everything was in order for my business and personal taxes at the end of the year. I have allowed her access to my business account, and weekly, she prepares a profit/loss statement to track all income and all expenses. Each week, she emails me my business reports with any questions she may have. I then email her within the week (sometimes longer) with my answers to her questions and any proposed revisions. This system makes me pay close attention to my finances on a weekly basis and keeps me organized. Because my bookkeeper works on my business accounts weekly, if there is a problem, we can have a discussion when the problem arises as opposed to trying to figure it out months later. She also ensures that all fees/taxes that I need to pay throughout the year are paid. At tax time, my bookkeeper sends the reports we have worked on all year to my accountant, and I am removed from the process until I need to review the taxes before filing. Easy.

When you begin your practice, you may opt to start with a program such as QuickBooks or Intuit to assist you with recordkeeping and scratch the bookkeeper in the beginning. If you know how to manage QuickBooks or a comparable program with ease, go for it. As you expand your business, you will ultimately decide if you need a bookkeeper or if you have the time to keep track of your earnings and spending and your taxes/fees. As my business grew, finances were one aspect that I did not want to mess up or worry about. Managing your income and inputting your expenses as you grow can consume a lot of time. My bookkeeper and I were able to negotiate a reasonable rate for her to manage my income/expenses remotely. With a small firm, I do not believe you need anyone full-time or in-office to complete this task. If you have a good bookkeeper, you will minimize the amount of time and energy spent with your tax consultant at the end of the year.

MANAGING BUSINESS INCOME/EXPENSES

1. How will I track my business income?

2. How will I track my business expenses?

3. Will I hire a part-time bookkeeper or do this myself?

6. BANK ACCOUNTS

You will need establish a business bank account that is separate from your personal accounts. I set up my business bank accounts at a different bank from my personal accounts (which is not necessarily a requirement), and I researched the best business account for my business. I wanted to have a personal relationship with my banker and have access to someone who could answer my questions and not require me to call an 800 number and wait to discuss my business with a stranger each time. That was important to me.

Some practice areas (like mine, Family Law) require a "client trust account" or an "IOTA" account (an account for collecting upfront fees/retainers). It is crucial that you are aware whether you are required to maintain an IOTA account and the proper steps for creating such an account. You want to also ensure that your bank is aware of the IOTA account and the proper setup with the State Bar.

7. BUSINESS CREDIT CARD

Do you need a business credit card? The answer to this question really depends on your cash flow and the size of your reserve accounts. There will be many unexpected expenses, courses you may want to attend, networking activities, and the list goes on. If you do not have a sizeable reserve account, you may want to consider the option of a business credit card for emergencies, especially when you initially start your business. Many banks offer great introductory rates when you open a business account, so if you need a business credit card, consider the options at the bank you select for your business accounts.

BANK ACCOUNTS AND CREDIT CARDS

1. *Where will I maintain my business bank account?*
2. *Do I need to maintain an IOTA account? Does my bank know how to properly set up the IOTA account?*
3. *Do I need a business credit card at this time?*

8. PAYROLL

Initially, you may only have yourself to worry about for payroll. But it is important to establish a routine to pay your salary, your taxes, and your expenses. If you decide to manage your business finances on your own, be sure to set up time each week, every other week, or every month to track all of your business-related expenses. In addition to the amount you will pay yourself and others, please be mindful of any payroll taxes required in your individual state.

PILLAR 3 – THE BUSINESS OF RUNNING YOUR LAW FIRM

Currently, I pay myself and my staff bi-weekly. My staff submits their time logs to my bookkeeper at least 48 hours prior to "pay day." My bookkeeper then notifies me of the "net" pay to pay my staff, and the taxes that must also be paid on their salaries and my own. The taxes are paid, my staff and I are paid, and everyone is happy.

PAYROLL

1. *How often will I pay myself and my staff?*
2. *Will I handle payroll, or will I hire someone to assist me?*
3. *How will I take care of my payroll taxes?*

9. MALPRACTICE INSURANCE

Unfortunately, especially in states like California, a client may sue you for legal malpractice for whatever reason. Such claims can consume a lot of your time and maybe your money. Legal malpractice insurance assists you in defending such claims and potentially assists with the cost of legal counsel if necessary. It is an added protection to your business, which is worth considering.

Initially, I did not purchase malpractice insurance. I was so new, and I did not want to incur the expense at the time. Because of my practice area (Family Law), I quickly learned from others that insurance was extremely necessary, if only limited insurance. When I did research, I learned that most companies offer affordable rates with decent coverage for attorneys who have been practicing for fewer than five years. The more you practice, the higher the premiums (assuming that you are likely to make more mistakes as you practice more). Just to ensure that you are covered for any potential claims, especially in areas such as Family Law, do research in this area to determine what makes the most financial and business sense for you and your practice.

In some states, if you do not carry malpractice insurance, you must disclose to your clients that you do not cover malpractice insurance.

In addition to legal malpractice insurance, some states also require that you maintain Workers' Compensation insurance if you have employees. Because I currently do have full-time employees, I maintain Workers' Compensation insurance, and I pay the premiums on a quarterly basis.

INSURANCE

1. *Will I maintain legal malpractice insurance?*

2. *If so, five companies in my area that offer affordable legal malpractice insurance are:*

    1) Company 1:

    2) Company 2:

    3) Company 3:

    4) Company 4:

    5) Company 5:

PILLAR 3 - THE BUSINESS OF RUNNING YOUR LAW FIRM

3. *Do I need Workers' Compensation insurance for my employees?*

4. *If so, five companies in my area that offer affordable Workers' Compensation insurance are:*

   1) Company 1:

   2) Company 2:

   3) Company 3:

   4) Company 4:

   5) Company 5:

PILLAR 4
Law Firm Management

What is the difference between "Business Management" and "Law Firm Management?" Business Management covers the basics to opening any business and the other legalities, as we discussed in Pillar 3. Law Firm Management covers what you specifically need to operate your law firm. The beauty is, you get to create your law firm as you see fit, and you can go as small or as big as you want.

I spent a considerable amount of time fumbling through law firm management before I finally found what worked best for me. Over the years, I have identified what I believe is important in forming and managing your law firm. Your practice may have additional steps that you want to cover in your personal plan, and please do not hesitate to include what is important to you. Here, I include the big topics that I consider to be a priority.

1. WHAT WILL THIS ALL COST ME? — THE BUDGET

When my law firm journey began, I started in my living room in my small apartment without an office, an assistant, clients, etc. I had my cell phone (and I believe I had a landline at the time), my computer with dial-up internet, and a credit card. No budget. I hoped and prayed I would earn enough money each month to cover my limited personal expenses at the time and my credit card expenses, which I incurred for business. What I can say with certainty is: KEEP YOUR EXPENSES AS LOW AS POSSIBLE. Repeat. KEEP YOUR EXPENSES AS LOW AS POSSIBLE.

When planning how you want your practice to look, first identify your fixed personal expenses, such as your rent, expenses for your family, personal utilities, student loan payments, and other miscellaneous expenses. Also, identify your personal flexible expenses, such as credit card payments. Once you know for sure what you will need to cover your personal expenses, also determine what you will need for your proposed business expenses, such as rent expense (if you decide to rent an office—we will cover this more), client costs, court costs, business taxes, payroll taxes, and any other specific business expenses to your firm. Once you have identified your personal and business expenses, you will know the minimum you need to earn each month to cover them.

WRITE THIS OUT

There is power in writing your expenses on paper and reviewing and adjusting as often as you need (weekly, monthly, quarterly, yearly). You always want to control the flow of money whenever you can, not the other way around.

PILLAR 4 - LAW FIRM MANAGEMENT

WHAT IF MY INITIAL INCOME DOES NOT COVER MY PERSONAL AND BUSINESS EXPENSES?

When I initially began my practice, I was single and 25 years old with no children, so I was only financially responsible for myself and the business.

Although I did not write out my expenses at the time, I did know that I needed to keep my expenses low. I initially incurred the expense each month to bid on clients (I paid for the most basic plan offered), the expenses to meet potential clients for coffee/lunch (RARELY, if ever, dinner), and the expense for letterhead and office materials. However, as the business began to slowly take off, the expenses grew, so at that time, I decided to create and manage a monthly business and personal budget. Within a year, I went from very few expenses to the expenses of renting an office, hiring staff (one paralegal and a part-time bookkeeper), and purchasing management software to meet the needs of the growing practice. Each time I experienced a major financial shift, I went back to the drawing board and adjusted my budget where possible.

Each month, especially in the beginning, is not smooth sailing. There were many months that I did not meet my income goals to cover both my personal and business expenses, and during those months, I had to prioritize what I would pay first and what expenses I would postpone. I did not have the privilege of access to reserves, but I would have felt much better if I did.

If you can start your practice with at least three months of reserves, then you'll have a good start, but the more money you have saved, the better, especially for those early months when you experience A LOT of highs and lows financially. There were times when I budgeted perfectly, but that did not mean that all clients paid on time. So, I had to adjust. The early months bring A LOT of uncertainty, so brace yourself.

Also remember that your goal is to be profitable, and although tempting, do not spend every dollar you earn. You want to continue to invest in your practice so that you can eventually earn what you want to earn, pay yourself top salary, and create reserves for a rainy day.

When you are planning, be honest about your personal expenses and what you can cover for your business expenses and consider what you will do in the event that you are unable to cover your expenses. Create your emergency plan just in case. Also consider whether you will apply for a personal loan, line of credit on your residence, or a new credit card. The more you have planned for the "unknown," the better you will feel should a slow month arise for you.

PILLAR 4

1. *What are my fixed personal expenses?*

2. *What are my adjustable personal expenses?*

3. *What are my business expenses?*

4. *What is my projected business income?*

5. *In the event I am unable to cover my expenses, then what?*

2. WHAT IS BILLING STRUCTURE?

Not all law firms charge by the hour, but hourly billing is still popular. In Los Angeles, the hourly rates can range from $250/hour to $1500/hour. I would not encourage you to start out at $1500 an hour, but funny story. When I initially started my practice, I met with a potential client, and I believe I quoted him $200/hour. I thought the meeting went great, and I just knew he would hire me. However, when I called to follow up on our meeting, he told me, "I'm sorry, but your rate is so low and not comparable to other rates that I have been quoted in the area. I can't hire you." Shocked, but great practice lesson! You want to be competitive in your market but still comparable to others with your experience and expertise.

From my experience, the sweet spot for Los Angeles attorneys in my practice area is anywhere from $350/hour and up largely based on your location, your practice area, your experience, and ultimately what your clients are willing to pay. Ask around if you are unsure. You not only want to know what others charge, but what clients are willing to pay.

Although the hourly fee structure is popular in many practice areas, there are other pay structures to consider. I have never really enjoyed the hourly fee structure and have tried different payment structures, such as a flat fee pay structure. I identified the major task for my business and determined an hourly rate based on the average number of hours it would take my office to complete the task. The problem with such a structure is that there was always additional unforeseen time spent, and clients did not want to deviate from the stated flat fee.

I also attempted a hybrid of hourly and flat fees, but at times it became more complicated to keep track of what was the hourly fee and what was the flat fee. If there is property involved, at least in Family Law, some attorneys will agree to be paid from the sale of the property, but that means receiving little compensation until the home is sold.

There are practice areas that also follow the contingency fee structure and collect fees based on what is earned during the case.

Bottom line: Do what works best for you.

Please understand you are running a business, and once you select your hourly rate or other fee structure, do not allow potential clients, family, friends, clients, and whoever needs your services to persuade you to lower your rates. There may be exceptions, but any deviation should ALWAYS be the exception and not the rule. I know we as women love to help others, but that does not mean we have to sacrifice our income to do so.

The same goes for collection. Do not allow clients, potential clients, etc. to run up their invoice with promises to pay. The truth is, if you do not collect as the case progresses, it is unlikely that you will be paid for your time. Again, you did not go into business to work for free. When you are planning for your billing system, be sure to incorporate a system for collection.

HOW MANY HOURS SHOULD I BILL EACH MONTH?

What is a good starting point for determining how many hours you should bill each month? Determine the income

PILLAR 4 - LAW FIRM MANAGEMENT

you want to earn for the month. Divide your desired income by your hourly rate. So for example, if you want to earn $25,000 a month to start, and your hourly rate is $250 an hour, you would divide $25,000 by $250 and the total billable hours for the month is 250 hours, which is approximately 62.5 hours a week. Wow! That is a lot of hours. If you do not have staff, and you do not want to work 62.5 hours a week, you may have to increase your hourly rate, or adjust your firm's income. Determine the absolute base income you need to clear your personal and business expenses and the hours you need to work to cover your expenses and go from that starting point.

BILLING STRUCTURE

1. *The hourly rate?*
2. *If so, what is my hourly rate?*
3. *A flat fee?*
4. *If so, what is my flat fee rate for each service that I provide?*
5. *How many hours should I bill each month?*

---

3. DO I CHARGE A RETAINER? PLEASE, PLEASE! AND IF SO, WHAT DO I PUT IN MY RETAINER AGREEMENT?

In various practice areas, attorneys require clients to pay a "retainer fee," an upfront payment to cover the initial hours of work to be expended on any given case. Some firms also require clients to replenish the retainer once depleted. The retainer can cover five (5) hours to twenty

(20) hours depending on the firm and the complexity of the case. In Family Law, attorneys charge anywhere from 10-25 hours (on average) for retainers, which can cost the client anywhere from $3,000 to $25,000 in upfront fees. The retainer allows you to work on your client's case, knowing you will receive immediate compensation for your work and not chasing your client to pay their invoice. The retainer does not alleviate the necessity for the monthly invoice; in fact, in most states it is required every month for the obvious reason that your client wants to know what you are charging and what has been expended.

Each state bar has specific rules surrounding the management of retainer fees, and most require attorneys to manage such fees in a separate account, better known as the "Trust Account." Each month as you bill your client and earn the fees, you are then allowed to transfer such fees out of the "Trust Account" into your operating business account. DO NOT, and I repeat, DO NOT mix your retainer account monies with your business/personal accounts.

4. RETAINER AGREEMENT.

If you do accept retainer fees, you will most likely have a retainer agreement. Your retainer agreement outlines the scope of your representation, your and your staff's fees, your required retainer agreement, client and firm expectations, the details for what occurs in the event of a dispute, and other conditions particular to your practice area. Your local bar may also specify what you can and cannot add to your retainer agreement and when you are required to have a retainer agreement (in most instances, when you have a

PILLAR 4 - LAW FIRM MANAGEMENT

case over $1,000). The retainer agreement is a great way for you to be clear on the scope of your representation and your exact expectations of the client. To alleviate any confusion, I require clients to initial after each paragraph of the retainer agreement.

You want to precisely draft your retainer in clear and simple terms for your client to understand. I know legalese sounds cool and all, but I have learned over the years that you would rather have your client understand the terms of your agreement instead of sounding cool.

There are many samples of retainer agreements online. Review the retainer agreements at your firm if you are at a firm, and ask your colleagues and friends if you can review their retainer agreements to get an idea of what you may or may not want to include. DO NOT copy what you receive but pay attention to what you like and potentially do not like in the retainer agreement. Over the years, I have changed my retainer agreement several times because as I grow, different concerns arise in the practice and new rules are released from the State Bar. It is good practice to get in the habit of regularly reviewing your retainer agreement as you grow in your practice.

RETAINER AND RETAINER AGREEMENT

1. Will I charge a retainer?

2. How much is my retainer?

3. Will I require full payment for the retainer, or will I accept payments?

4. *Does my firm require a retainer agreement?*

5. *What are the terms of my retainer agreement?*

5. WHAT IS MY PRACTICE AREA?

Luckily, I did enjoy the practice of Family Law for the six months that I worked for the first law firm. When I started my practice, I did not consider adding a different area or consider changing my practice area. I considered and tried Bankruptcy for a short period of time because so many clients do need a Bankruptcy attorney after going through a challenging divorce. Bankruptcy was more paperwork than Family Law, so I ditched Bankruptcy. I also considered Trusts, Wills, and Estate Planning and even paid for an expensive course to determine if I was interested. I was not. After trying both Bankruptcy and Trusts, Wills, and Estates, I realized Family Law was best for me.

Planning the opening your own law practice is good time to assess if you enjoy your current practice area or if you want to try something new. That is the beauty of having a law degree—you do not have to stick to one practice area if you do not enjoy it. I know several attorneys who started their practice in completely new areas of the law. Whatever you decide, just decide. DO NOT try to be a "jack of all trades." Pick no more than three (and three is a lot) practice areas to focus on. Once you have identified your area of practice, vow to become the "go to" person for that area of law. I encourage you to go further and pick a specific "niche" in your area, for example, Family Law for fathers in your area, Employment Law for single mothers, etc. Once you know your area of practice, then you will do just that, practice and practice until you become the expert.

PRACTICE AREA

1. *What is my practice area?*

2. *Do I want to change my practice area?*

3. *What other areas do I want to consider?*

   1) Area 1:

   2) Area 2:

   3) Area 3:

---

6. PARTNER OR NO PARTNER?

Okay. So, I tried this. Twice. And partnership, at least in the traditional sense, is not for me. The first time, I partnered with someone from the same practice area. After a few meetings, I believed that we had "enough" in common to make the partnership work (we practiced in the same practice area, we got along well, we had both been practicing for about the same amount of time, and we had mutual respect), but it ended up that we were still too different to work together. After a few months, we both realized the partnership did not work. The problem with this first partner from my perspective was that she was new to "business," and she just wanted to practice law and did not fully understand the business of running the practice, and it really did not interest her.

I, on the other hand, wanted an actual partner, not an associate, and by that time, I had spent enough time practicing to know that we had to run the business just as much as we had to practice law. I learned extremely fast that "enough" commonalities will not sustain a successful partnership. It is important to have similar goals, practice styles, and an understanding of business and law firm management that complement one another and a detailed understanding of your roles. I did not have that with my first partner, so if I am now transparent, our foundation was weak from the start. I did not know how to assess her understanding and willingness to work on the business, not just in the business, her business management skills, or her law firm management skills. I just knew she was a decent lawyer, nice, and our personalities seemed to match. But that was simply not enough.

Dissolving the partnership was also a mess for me. I decided at the time to revise all my marketing materials seven years in the making to reflect the new partnership. Not the best decision for me. I then incurred the cost of changing everything back to my solo firm after we dissolved the partnership. Not fun, but I learned a lot, and I moved on.

I learned from that partnership that you must really get to know your partner and understand both of your strengths and weaknesses. Really identify your respective roles, all the way down to marketing, payment to each partner, experience, and the expectations for both and also to consider a partnership agreement to really detail what should occur in the event that either party wants to dissolve a partnership. I have witnessed some pretty ugly showdowns

PILLAR 4 – LAW FIRM MANAGEMENT

between partners, so be prepared to discuss EVERYTHING just as you would if you were getting married.

Okay. When the second partnership opportunity presented itself, I thought I was ready because I had learned how to "partner" from the first failed experience. This time, I tried something "bigger and better," and I did not convert my firm, but started a second firm (I vividly remember the stress of merging my firm from before, and I just could not do that again). It was a great idea, an all-women-owned firm, and we incorporated other professionals to cover the needs that arose from our representation (PR, mental health services, and financial services). We started off great. A lot of media attention, strong presence. But this partnership also failed within a year.

This time, we did have the same goal of seeing the business succeed, but we were simply not a good fit. From my perspective, she was younger than I was by several years (for this situation in particular, this mattered because with continued practice comes experience, and our experience levels were very different), our management styles were very different, and our client management styles were very different. Our clientele was also very different. Unfortunately, management styles are ridiculously hard to observe until you are in the partnership, and the same goes with experience.

We did not share the same philosophies for running our business, managing the other professionals, and overall practicing law. It was also challenging because if I introduced a client to the new firm, that client still largely wanted only me to service their file, so that was challenging during times when I wanted to handle other matters. Needless to say, we tried for some time, but this partnership also failed.

Transitioning back to just my own practice was much better this time around. I did not convert my business this time, so returning to just my private practice was a much smoother transition.

Bottom line: Partnerships do not work for me (at least the last two did not).

But partnerships DO work for others.

A good friend and fellow Family Law attorney LOVES her partnership (you will read about her in the final pillar). Her partnership works for her because she has identified what she needs to make the partnership work, and she and her partner have been able to create a practice that mirrors both of their visions. In this situation, my friend is comfortable with litigation, going to court, meeting clients, and handling potential clients, and her partner drafts the necessary paperwork, court documents, briefs, letters to clients, etc. It works for her. If you can find a good fit, partnerships can be successful and alleviate some stress for you.

That is key. Finding the right fit if you want a partner and really discussing everything surrounding not just the firm, practice areas, etc., but the business of the firm, personalities, likes/dislikes, expectations, and business and law firm philosophies. Also consider a probationary period of three to six months to see if the partnership is right for you and to observe if you have the right partner. It reminds me a lot of dating. LOL. You might not know exactly what you like or

PILLAR 4 - LAW FIRM MANAGEMENT

do not like until the partnership begins. Please remember, you will be required to spend a lot of time discussing money and work with your partner, probably more than you do with your own significant other, so it is crucial to select wisely.

PARTNERSHIPS

1. Will I have a partner?

2. Why or why not?

3. How will I select my partner?

4. Potential partners:

    1) Potential partner 1:

    2) Potential partner 2:

    3) Potential partner 3:

---

7. DO I NEED AN OFFICE?

In the beginning, I did not have an office for an entire year. And I was fine.

During the early months of my practice, if I needed to meet potential clients in person, I would travel to a local Starbucks or small restaurant (during lunch hours for cost purposes) of the potential client's selecting. Some clients want to ensure that you are a real person. But a large majority of clients do not request an in-person meeting and opt to consult with and speak to the attorney and complete case paperwork via email/website, Zoom, or other online means.

After a year of practicing from my home, I rented a small interior office space in a local corporate office—you know, the one that charges you for everything from postage, to coffee fees, etc. Corporate office spaces charge for EVERYTHING, or at least this has been my experience. I incurred costs from "beverage fees" to drink the coffee and tea (yes, I drank a lot of coffee and tea), "fees" to send out email, "fees" to fax, which of course is on top of the rent, which tends to fluctuate at least 10-20% each renewal period.

I selected the office because it was close to my residence at the time, literally within walking distance. I also did not have a large client base to consider when deciding if the location was right for my practice. Most corporate offices also offer conference room space, parking, etc. Once I rented the office, I no longer had to travel around Los Angeles County to meet new clients. However, although I was earning more consistent money, I had added a big expense to have the office.

Currently, my office is surviving the infamous coronavirus pandemic, and my entire staff and I are working remotely. All of our files our stored in a web-based program, and we complete our client forms on a web-based program that allows all of us access to case forms if necessary. Honestly, we did experience a few "adjustment pains" in the beginning, but we are managing just fine. We can fax files and all other documents to the court, and in the foreseeable future, we will be able to electronically file our documents. Some states have already begun the process for electronic filing, but my county is a little slower because of its size and needed updates to an outdated court system. I

PILLAR 4 - LAW FIRM MANAGEMENT

can also appear for my court hearings telephonically from the comfort of my home office.

Because of advances in technology, an office is no longer as major a necessity for law firms as it once was. Before my staff and I were forced to work from home, I had rented two office spaces from a corporate rental and a "satellite" office located in a different city. I pay approximately $170.00 per month for the "satellite" office. This fee includes answering any calls and collecting mail in addition to the use of the office space. For our physical offices, I pay over $3,000 per month for two office spaces, and that includes phone service, parking, etc. However, in the age of the internet, major advancements in technology, etc., and the reality of telecommuting, $3,000 for office needs is excessive.

I do enjoy separating my work life from my home life, but because I still understand the need to adjust office expenses when and if necessary, I have to find ways to accomplish my goal of getting out of the house, but not spending so much money on office space.

Many corporate offices now provide varying office packages which include the main necessities: answering your phones and transferring your calls to whatever contact number you select, collecting your mail, and providing conference room space and day offices, if needed, for far less than $3,000 per month.

You ultimately know what works best for you, but it is crucial to consider all possibilities and determine what your office needs are before deciding to commit your money and be locked into unnecessary office space.

IS THE LOCATION OF MY OFFICE IMPORTANT?

Because of technology, etc., office location is not as important as it once was. I do not believe location is as determinative of a client's hiring you as it was when I initially started practicing (unless someone just really wants a Beverly Hills attorney or someone specific to their area). My main office is located primarily in Pasadena, California, and most of my clients (80%) come from all over Los Angeles County. I do maintain a satellite office in Beverly Hills just in case my clients in that area want to meet, but this is rarely an issue. As mentioned, most of my conferences are done telephonically, and now video conferencing is becoming increasingly popular.

Also consider where you have most of your court hearings as that is a major consideration if traveling is of concern to you.

You know your practice area. If you are concerned about the location of your office, research your area of expertise to determine if "office location" is a determining factor for clients in your field. I would still suspect, especially after the ever-changing coronavirus pandemic, that office location is not as important as the outstanding services that you provide.

OFFICE SPACE/LOCATION

1. *Do I need additional office space?*
2. *Can my office operate remotely?*
3. *What is the best office location for my firm?*

PILLAR 4 - LAW FIRM MANAGEMENT

8. STAFF VS. NO STAFF.

Remember, you want to keep expenses down as much as possible and hiring employees will cost you. In addition to your employees' salary, you will also pay payroll taxes and other benefits you provide. You will be required to manage their work and manage personalities. The goal is to ensure the cases are serviced the way you want based on the training you will provide.

Starting out, I did not have a book of business when I opened my practice, and I started from scratch with zero clients, so I did everything myself: answering the phones, client intake, client meetings, completing the court forms, document filing, and, of course, the legal work associated with each case and all court appearances. Of course, when the business began to grow, I needed help! I did not want to spend a lot of money because I was not earning a lot of money, and I always remembered my motto, KEEP EXPENSES LOW. But I did want the business to continue to grow, and I wanted to have a little flexibility to attend networking meetings, Bar meetings, etc.

I began to consider where I could use the most help. Because Family Law is heavily form-based, I decided that I needed someone to assist with client management and completing the case forms. I hired a part-time assistant to prepare documents, schedule phone conferences between me and clients, manage mail, and calendar all court hearings and client appointments. Keeping cost in mind, I hired someone whom I could train to complete the tasks as I wanted them done and someone whom I could afford. Some attorneys do not want to spend a lot of time training and would prefer to pay for experience. With experience comes a much higher salary.

As I earned more money and the firm grew, I eventually hired my assistant full-time. As the office grew, and the tasks of the firm grew, I then hired a part-time file clerk to manage the client files. I watched the practice closely as the firm grew, and when I needed assistance, I hired help. You will know if and when you need assistance. Hire based on your firm's needs, not based on what others suggest you need.

When you start your practice, you might start from the ground up, as I did, or you might begin with business and financial resources, which may allow you to hire the staff you need for your practice. But again, start with what you absolutely need to open your doors, and you can later add additional staff as the business and your financial resources grow. Ignore what you have seen on TV or have heard others say about all their "associates" and shiny law firm objects, etc. Do what is best for YOU.

How Much Do I Pay These People?
I Have To Give You The Lawyer Answer: It Depends

You want someone who is competent, follows directions, adopts your firm's culture and philosophies, gets the work done, and maybe most importantly, gets along with others. With that said, what do you pay your staff? I had no clue what to pay my first assistant. Because of my limited budget, I decided to hire someone new to the legal field who wanted to learn and whom I could train. I researched the salary for an entry-level legal assistant, and I asked my colleagues. Based on my research and the information obtained from my colleagues, my assistant and I settled on a part-time hourly rate that allowed her to assist me and obtain another job if necessary. We agreed to revisit her salary after six months (which included the three-month probationary period) and decide if she was a fit for the firm and to discuss her salary based on her progress.

The upside of hiring someone with limited experience is the opportunity to train them to write your letters and prepare your documents exactly the way you like, answer your calls the way you want, etc. The downside is the time commitment to train someone how to do everything you want done. As my assistant learned more, and it was evident that we worked well together, I did continue to increase her salary and increase her hours. As the firm grew, her hours and pay increased.

This continues to be my practice today with anyone whom I hire. I hire to address a rising need in the practice, the starting salary is comparable to the new hire's experience, and the salary increases with time if the hire is a fit for the practice.

Just FYI, I would caution you to pay well your staff who have proven to be a good fit for your firm! I will say that good support staff is hard to come by. You can also consider paying for schooling or a certificate for your staff. The gesture goes a long way. I paid for two of my assistants to obtain their paralegal license. They were so grateful and remained in the firm for what I believe was a longer period of time because of the gesture (or maybe they needed a job, LOL). Either way, it worked.

I have found that if you are good to staff, your staff will also be good to you. This is not to imply that you should break the bank, but do pay your staff well and treat them with respect, always. They work for you, yes, but they are still deserving of your respect.

Another way to employ assistance for your firm for reasonable compensation is to hire law clerks, law students who eagerly want to gain experience in your area of expertise. Most law students are required to meet specific practical hours to graduate, and some law schools will pay students a stipend, etc. Most law students are available for summer positions (6-8 weeks of cost-effective work for your firm), and as law students reach 2L-3L status, the hours are often extended. I had great success with law clerks—one of the best workers I ever had was a law clerk. I was devastated when she decided to take a job out of state after law school, which was for the best because I probably would have financially overextended myself to hire her.

9. FIRM BENEFITS OR NOT?

I know the cost of health insurance and retirement benefits has greatly increased over the last few years, but if possible, offering benefits is another way to entice good workers to come and remain with your firm. So many companies, law firms included, have dumped additional benefits because of cost, but if you have the option to offer benefits, your firm becomes more enticing to good employees.

EMPLOYEES

1. *Do I need to hire employees right now?*

PILLAR 4 - LAW FIRM MANAGEMENT

2. *If so, whom do I need to hire?*

    1) Employee 1:

    2) Employee 2:

    3) Employee 3:

3. *How much will I pay each employee?*

---

10. SYSTEMS. SYSTEMS. SYSTEMS.

You always want to run your business and not allow the business to run you. There is so much to manage and so much to do. Before I really understood the importance of all the pieces of business and law firm ownership and really took control, my business was running me.

How do you make sure you are in control and stay in control? Establish systems for each part of the business of the firm and the practice management aspect of your firm. Once you establish your systems, you can then assign management of your systems to your staff, or you can manage your own systems.

Systems are key and will make your law firm run smoother and save you a lot of headaches. Another great benefit of managing your own firm is that you have the autonomy to create your own systems and identify what works best for you. It took me some time to really identify the best systems for the firm, and those systems sometimes change, or we revamp the system, etc. But your goal is to establish systems that work best for you; they do not have to be extra fancy.

What are the main systems that you should consider when you first open your practice? Again, this is based on my experience and what I have found to work best. Please do not hesitate to revise the list that I have provided or find other systems that work better for you.

1. **Client Management System.** There are extremely complicated client management systems and other not so complicated systems. Over time, I identified what I needed in my practice and researched as many systems as I could to decide the best system for my firm. Of course, there are always the famous programs that your previous firm used and that the attorneys in your area use, but I encourage you do your own research to determine what works best for you. I wanted a simple, cost-effective program that covered the entire client experience from the first potential call to the conclusion of the case in a simple format that my staff and I could understand. I wanted to use just one program rather than several different programs to manage our clients (which I did in the past). Our client management system simplified the mundane tasks in the firm (adding potential clients, conflict checks, etc.) and also simplified the more complicated areas (calendaring, forms, etc.). The cost of an effective client management system can run anywhere from $100 a month up to $20,000 a month depending on your firm's needs and how complicated you want your system to be.

2. **Calendaring.** You want a great calendaring system. My office currently maintains all dates in our master calendar on our client management system and a Google calendar. I also keep a paper calendar to make sure I do

PILLAR 4 - LAW FIRM MANAGEMENT

not miss court dates, deadlines, and other important meetings. As soon as we receive a court date from the court, opposing counsel, or other sources, all dates are immediately added to all calendars and my paper calendar. Your management program should definitely have a calendaring function.

3. Billing. The dreadful task of billing. Our client management system allows us to bill from the system. But you still must do it! LOL. I believe that one day there will be a better way to be paid for our services, but currently we still bill hourly for our services. Please also note that you will not always receive what you bill, so pay close attention each month to the percentage of what you actually have received from the billable time, and that way, you can increase or decrease what your monthly earnings will be.

My staff and I update our billable hours daily (for the most part), and I check the firm's time weekly. Each week, I check everyone's time (including my own time) to ensure that we are meeting our firm's goals. Also, making sure we all input our time as we go alleviates the headache at the end of the month. Our management system also allows us to input time from our cell phones, which is helpful if we are on the go. We send out monthly bills to our clients on the 5th day of each month. Our clients can then pay their invoices directly in the system, and I do not have to worry about crediting their account; and each client can view all invoices or payments submitted and any outstanding balances in the system.

4. Conflict Check. In most practice areas, you want to ensure that you have not spoken to the other side of a potential case. Most programs allow you to insert the name of the other party to do a conflict check before you schedule any potential meetings, etc.

5. Form Completion. Family Law is heavily form-based. In many counties, the forms are located online if you do not wish to pay for a form completion program, but the online forms do not save the information that you repeatedly use such as your name, bar number, firm name, firm address, and firm contact information. The free online forms are doable but repetitive. There are several companies that offer form preparation services. Some programs are housed on your computer (not always compatible with Apple, etc.), which limits your access at times, for example, between home and work. Most recently our firm switched to a web-based program that allows you to access your form library from anywhere, which makes sense if you and your staff need constant access to your firm's forms. I used the desktop forms for many years, which are housed on only one computer if the computers are not networked. I found that my staff had to constantly print out the forms for my review, I would make corrections, and they would re-print the forms until we had everything right. We were wasting time, paper, and money. Now with the web-based forms, I can review the forms at my leisure and print them out when they are file-ready. Also, if your computer crashed for whatever reason, you would be out of luck without a web-based form preparer. The price of document preparation course can also range anywhere from $600 a year on up.

6. Storing Client Information. Like our form completion software, we also use a web-based storage system for storing all client data accumulated over the life of the case. We also can send our clients a link to their entire client file. Web-based storage and drives can range anywhere from $25 dollars or so per month up to $100 per month, depending on which drive you select.

7. Closed Client Files. Each state has identified how long you must store a client file once you complete the case. Because files can easily pile up, I rented a small storage space to house these closed case files. Once their time is up, I pay a shredding company to shred the files and make room for other files. Storage space can also range from $45 per month up to $500 per month, depending on the size of the storage unit.

I have identified my top seven systems that will make any firm run so much easier. You may find that you need additional systems for your business and forego some of the identified systems above, and that is okay. You must always do what is best for you and your bank account. The goal is to streamline your practice as much as possible to allow you the time to practice law. When you have identified your firm's systems, it is so much easier to know where you need staff to manage each step of the process and a clear way to understand how the business is progressing.

SYSTEMS

1. *What systems do I need for my practice?*

   1)

   2)

   3)

   4)

   5)

   6)

   7)

II. PROFESSIONAL DEVELOPMENT.

You want to stay on top of your game in your field. In addition to managing your business and practicing law, you must also find time for professional development. What does that even mean? Every year, many organizations host continuing education programs for you to learn about the newest laws or practice pointers or hot topics. Yes, you need your continuing education credits to report to the bar, but it is also useful to ensure that you are current on the law, especially when there are major changes in your practice area.

In most states, there is also the opportunity to "specialize" in one or more area of the law. Check your state bar's website to determine if specialization is offered in your state and your field. Once you pass a one-day exam, you can

PILLAR 4 - LAW FIRM MANAGEMENT

then hold yourself out as a "specialist" (at least that is the case in California). As a specialist, you can also join other specialists and attend additional seminars, etc. I also find that specialization raises your credibility and shows that you are committed to your field. Clients who are aware of the specialization also seek out a specialist in the field in which they are seeking counsel.

PROFESSIONAL DEVELOPMENT

1. *How will I continue to professionally advance my career?*

    1)

    2)

    3)

    4)

    5)

    6)

    7)

PILLAR 5

Marketing

Allow me to let you in on a little secret: marketing is your business. If you do not market your practice, and your potential clients do not know how to find you, you will not have a business. You can be the best attorney in the world, Number 1 in your law school class, and have the best suites in the world, but if people are unable to find you, it will not matter. To have a successful business, you will need to spend ample time marketing your services, especially in the beginning.

In my opinion, there are two prongs of marketing. One is your personal brand, your name, who you are, your reputation, how you present to the world, how you present to the legal community, and how you present to the court, if you are a litigator. How you walk it, talk it, dress it. For instance, I practice Family Law. I wanted to be the "go-to" Family Law attorney or at least one of the "go-to" Family Law attorneys in my area. So, what did I do to assist with my brand? I went to every continuing education course I could afford to ensure that I was current on the law and that I presented well in court. When I was eligible, I became a

"Certified Family Law Specialist," and I joined several Family Law-specific boards. In doing so, I received the education I needed to stay current, meet other colleagues in my area, and further my personal brand.

The other prong of marketing is getting your services in front of those who need your services right away, will eventually need your services, or know others who need/will need your services. What does that look like? The way you market is totally up to you, and there are so many ways to get your name out there, but this is what I believe you can do immediately. It is crucial to identify your ideal client, and then you go to where your ideal clients are to find them. This is so much easier now than it was before. When I started, everyone was fighting for a million-dollar website and placement in the Yellow Pages. That is old news now. The internet is forever changing and providing new and improved opportunities to market your services.

WHAT ARE WAYS YOU CAN MARKET YOUR SERVICES?

Identify Your Ideal Client: Before you begin searching for your client, you first need to identify your ideal client. Who is this person? What do they look like? What is the need or problem you will address? Are they a certain age? Do they hang out anywhere specifically? What other services do they already utilize? After several years of practice, I began to keep a list of the clients I really loved to work with, the clients who really wanted to resolve their cases and not "fight" over every issue, big and small. Clients who had the financial resources to litigate if possible, but to also understand the importance of resolving the matter rather than litigating just

PILLAR 5 - MARKETING

to litigate. Most of my ideal clients have been married 8 years plus, may or may not have children, and are professionals. In the beginning, I had no clue what I liked, so it took me some time to refine the profile of the client with whom I wanted to work. As you grow in your practice, your ideal client may also change several times. But when you are preparing to market your law firm, you want some understanding of whom you are marketing to.

Referral Partners: Establish a network with other attorneys who do not specialize in your practice area or who do practice in your area but are unable to take a case for whatever reason. "Qualified" potential clients are the best potential clients because someone has already vouched for your services, and the potential client already knows you do good work before they even contact you. Identify your friends, colleagues, associates, and old law school buddies who you can contact to become mutual referral partners. This strategy is a great way to receive and give business. Be sure to thank your referral partners and express your gratitude, and when applicable, refer clients back to your referral partners. A lot of attorneys forego many other forms of marketing because they have a strong referral network.

Social Media: What a lot of attorneys have now that we did not have at this level when I first started my practice is social media: Facebook, Instagram, YouTube, not TikTok. A large majority of the world spends a considerable amount of time browsing social media. Many attorneys also place ads on social media, start and manage groups for their potential and actual clients, have individual pages for their law firms, create videos, and the list continues. Social media is a great way to showcase your talents, your firm, and your success in your practice area. You are not always selling yourself, but you are always providing useful content to stay relevant for your potential clients and for others to identify you as the expert. The days of "I have over X amount of years of experience in whatever practice area" is over. People want to know how you can assist them in solving their problem—everything else is secondary. Also, befriend attorneys in other practice areas and in other cities and states because they may very well become part of your referral network.

Website: Most attorneys I know still create websites to have a presence on the web. Websites were far more popular and utilized in 2005 than they are now. When I finally created a website for my practice, I went with the company all attorneys used and I paid to have what all the other attorneys had in an attempt to be "competitive." But I was not competitive at all. I just ended up looking like every other attorney out there. You want to stand out, not look like everyone else. You want to have your own look, your own style, etc. I like to say, find what everyone else is doing, and do the total opposite. You also do not have to spend thousands of dollars on a website because there are so many other places for your clients to locate you, like social media. When I was starting out, "Google Ads" and other pay-per-click services were extremely popular, meaning you would pay for top placement on Google and other sites, and you would pay every single time someone clicked on your website. Again, I suppose others still utilize Google Ads, but there are other ways to showcase your business without spending thousands of dollars on a website. You can organically grow your website with constant up-to-date content, videos, and longevity.

PILLAR 5 - MARKETING

YouTube: Videos seem to be the wave of the future. If you search on YouTube, you will find many attorneys with helpful 1–2 minute tips in their respective practice areas. The key is to provide useful content and keep your firm at the top of your potential client's mind when the "problem" arises. You can create a video for your firm and place the link on your social media pages, YouTube channel, and your website for maximum exposure. The key with YouTube is consistency and encouraging your clients, potential clients, and family and friends to subscribe to your channel.

Podcast: If you do not enjoy being in front of the camera, you can consider podcasting your information for your potential and actual clients. You can create a weekly/bi-weekly/monthly broadcast that you can in turn add to your YouTube page, your website, and your social media outlets. This is a great way to get content out to your ideal clients.

Firm Newsletter: To stay in constant contact with your clients, a firm newsletter with new laws, a firm update, a seasonal recipe, and whatever you want to share is also a nice touch to keep in contact with your prior, present, and potential clients.

There are countless ways to market to always grow your brand and find ways to get your firm in front of those who need your services. As you decide what works best for you and your firm, your marketing plan may change several times until you find something that you really enjoy. For starters, identify how you plan to: 1) Brand yourself, your name, and your reputation; and 2) "Market" the business.

As you can imagine, marketing can be a full-time career. If you do not have anyone to manage your marketing for you, it is important to designate time to make sure that your marketing plan is implemented and that you are making any necessary changes. You always want to stay on top of your marketing.

PILLAR 5

1. *What is my brand marketing plan?*

2. *How will I market the practice?*

    1)

    2)

    3)

    4)

    5)

PILLAR 6

Client Management

Client management begins at the time you receive the first potential call. From the onset, you will teach your potential and actual clients how your firm operates. You are not obligated to take calls at all hours of the day and night. You want to be accessible and return all calls, but you decide how you will service your clients in a way that is responsive to your clients but also allows you time to complete all your tasks.

When I started out, potential clients and actual clients called my cell phone all hours of the day and night. Because I failed to set the boundaries at the onset of the relationship, I felt I needed to talk to clients right away. However, this eventually became exhausting, and I found myself talking on the phone more than I worked. Now, I have an answering service that answers all calls, and the calls are then filtered to either my paralegal, someone else on my staff, or, on rare occasions, to me. If a potential client would like to schedule time for a consultation, I now charge for my consultation time (you can spend all day long speaking to potentials) in 15- and 30-minute increments. Most of my current client calls are scheduled on my calendar unless, of course, there is an emergency that we need to handle right away. I have a dedicated cell phone just for work (this was created because of the COVID pandemic and the necessity for me to separate personal and work calls). I also turn off my work phone between the hours of 7:00 p.m. and 8:00 a.m. to ensure that I do not continue to work past my designated working hours.

Prior to creating boundaries, I often felt like my firm was bossing me around and that I was not in control of the practice. Once I changed how I interacted with clients and potential clients, I was able to have much more control of my schedule during the day. Each day, I block out time for my staff to schedule calls for me. Of course, there are emergencies, and I must take calls right away, but otherwise all calls with clients, potential clients, opposing counsel, and others are scheduled based on my daily availability.

Once a client contacts your firm, three things happen: 1) they hire you; 2) they do not hire you; or 3) they take time to think about it and then call you back and hire you, after most likely calling around the city to talk to other attorneys, and if the client is not a "qualified lead," price shopping. You need a system in place for each possibility.

Once a client hires our firm, the next step is to add the client to our client management system, complete initial paperwork (retainer agreement and intake firm) and instruct our client how to upload any documents to the management system. My staff will then send a welcome email addressing all next steps and what our client can

PILLAR 6 – CLIENT MANAGEMENT

expect during the process. We set the expectations early and attempt to provide the client with all pertinent information before they have to ask. The day the client says "yes," we establish boundaries and lay out the game plan from the beginning. This process is led by our client management system so that we do not forget where we are for each client.

My firm also schedules a strategy call between me and the client to discuss how we will proceed with their case. This step is done after they have received an email explaining firm expectations and their immediate next steps. The strategy we outline during our strategy call is then emailed to our client, so that the client is aware of what to expect as it relates to the strategy of their case going forward. I find that the strategy call and email provide the client with a roadmap for their case and help us manage expectations.

If a potential client is a "maybe," we also arrange in our client management system for me or my staff to follow up with the potential client over the next six (6) weeks or until the client informs us that they would like to proceed with our firm, do not need our services, or have decided to go with another firm. Follow-up is key for the "maybe" clients, and my office has received several clients from simply following up after the initial consultation. Once the potential client informs us of their decision, we document to the client their decision regarding services and close out the potential client file.

If a potential client says "no," we send an email confirming that the client has declined services (just to ensure there is no gray area or misunderstanding of representation).

YOUR FIRST CLIENT

On July 5, 2005, the first day of my practice, I did not have one client, one lead, nothing—I really started from scratch. If this business was going to work, I needed clients, or I was going to crash and burn faster than I had anticipated. Remember—if clients do not know who you are or what you offer, you have no business. Before my opening day, I should have spent the time implementing some form of marketing plan, which I clearly did not do. As I researched the best way to get legal clients, I found a service which allows you to "bid" on clients in your practice area for a monthly fee. I did not have much money at the time, but I did sign up and throw the expense on my credit card with hopes that I would at least start building my practice with clients I was able to win based on my bids.

Over the next couple of days, I submitted my bids for clients, low-balling my hourly rate, essentially taking whatever I could get, and basically begging! I do not recommend this method. Because at the time I did not know how to price my services, and I had not spent time marketing, I was somewhat desperate. This type of "marketing" can be avoided if you spend time before you open your doors notifying your book of business if you have business, notifying your family, friends, and potential referral partners, and beginning your marketing plan. You also want to set a competitive rate for your services.

Despite my low hourly rate, I did slowly begin to win bids on clients. Yes. I went to trial over a refrigerator and old cars. Yes. A lot of the clients did not have money to even pay my very under-market fee. But I must say that I did in fact learn a lot

PILLAR 6 – CLIENT MANAGEMENT

about the clients whom I wanted to have, and I did not want to ruin my reputation with the types of cases that I did have, so after a few disasters in the bidding game, I started to be more cautious of the clients for whom I bid, and I was forced to raise my hourly rate to attempt to change my clientele.

The process of getting my first client was extremely slow because I did not have a book of business, and ultimately, I did not do what I should have done. So, it took some time to build the momentum of having a stream of clients with the resources to pay for my services. Please do not get discouraged if the influx of clients is slow, especially if you do not have clients when you open your doors. Keep letting others know what you do, create and follow your marketing plan, and the clients will eventually come.

Also, do not stop marketing your business when you start retaining clients. Keep the pipeline full, at least to your firm's capacity. You always want to strive to have a steady flow of clients.

PILLAR 6

1. *Do I have a book of business, or do I need to start from the beginning?*
2. *How many clients will I have the day I open my doors?*
3. *How will I manage potential clients and clients?*
4. *What is my system for all potential clients?*
5. *What is my system for scheduling potential clients?*
6. *What is my system for the client that wants to retain my firm?*

7. *What is my system for the client that wants to think about hiring my firm?*

8. *What is the close out process for the client who did not hire my firm?*

PILLAR 7

The Court Experience: You're on Your Own Now...

Okay, for us litigators, court is a BIG DEAL. So, what can you expect when you are the boss, creating the strategies and going to court, what is this like?

In addition to managing the business of running a law office, managing the law practice, and practicing law, now you also have to manage your court calendar and prepare to attend court anywhere from zero to five (5) days a week.

At my very first court appearance, I was a nervous wreck. But luckily, at the time, I was still at my first job and able to attend the hearing with a more experienced attorney. The night before, I did not get much sleep. I really did not know what to expect, how the court process worked, or what I should wear.

I decided to prepare my first court outfit the night before. A lot of attorneys do not dress up like you see on TV, but I still believe you should wear that suit and nice shoes and look presentable and respectful to the court.

I learned prior to my first appearance that most courts open at 8:30 a.m., meaning I should actually arrive at 8:00 a.m. (I so do not do this now, but this is what I believed at the time) to park and walk at least half of a mile to the court and then navigate my way to my department for the day. I was of course much earlier my first day; because of my nerves, I was unable to sleep, and I did not know how the traffic would be (you never know with LA traffic). Once I arrived and parked ($20.00 to park), I made my way to the court doors, which required me to walk through metal detectors (please leave your nail files or your knives or whatever you carry for protection in your purse, in your car, or at home and save yourself the embarrassment).

After you pass the metal detectors, you now have the task of locating your department. In a smaller court, this may not be an issue, but in a large court (like our central court in downtown Los Angeles) this can be a task. Luckily, most courts have directories right at the entrance to assist you in identifying the room and floor of your department.

Once you locate your department, there is typically a bailiff or a clerk that collects your business card and asks which case you are appearing for. Your client may or may not be present. If necessary, courts require you to "meet and confer" with opposing counsel to determine if there are any matters to discuss prior to the hearing or any attempt to resolve the issue(s) or at least narrow the issues if possible. After that entire process, then you wait until your matter is called. You can wait 2–3 hours for your case to be called

PILLAR 7 – THE COURT EXPERIENCE

to appear before the judge for 15-20 minutes, the hurry up and wait game.

What I learned over the years is that there is a fine line between being assertive and advocating for your client and being disrespectful and unprofessional. Even if you are in fact being a strong advocate, women are quicker to be labeled "aggressive" and other less desirable names.

The first day that I appeared in court, I did not have to say a word in open court because the parties agreed to settle their matter before seeing the judge (phew!).

The first time that I appeared in court and had to speak on behalf of the client and everything was on my shoulders, I appeared in front of a well-known judge, notorious for embarrassing attorneys on the record in front of their clients. Terrified is an understatement. Luckily, I was prepared and ready for anything, and I did not get yelled at in front of my client. THANK GOD!

KNOW YOUR JUDGE! Ask your colleagues, go to your department prior to your hearing, and observe how the judge handles their calendars. Pay close attention to what the judge likes and dislikes, study their demeanor, observe how counsel treat each other and treat the court (including the court's clerk).

If you did not attend many court appearances before opening your firm, going to court can be extremely scary because you do not know what to expect. Like anything else, the more you appear in court, observe the court proceedings, and become more comfortable, court will not be as scary and intimidating as time goes on.

Navigating the courtroom as a woman is eye-opening. Women attorneys are still often mistaken for court staff, secretaries, assistants, defendants, etc. When I first started practicing, I remember appearing in court on one of my cases, and while I was waiting in line with the rest of the attorneys to check in, the woman clerk asked me, "Are you the court reporter checking in?"

I politely smiled, and said, "No, I'm here on case number (stated the case number)." She gave me an, "Oh," with no apology. No acknowledgment, just "Oh." Now granted, I was younger and maybe I looked lost, but then I thought would you have said that to a younger male or white male? I know that court reporters are typically women. But to assume that I was the court reporter in line with other attorneys did not sit right with me. In that moment, I remember thinking, okay, when circumstances such as these arise, how will I respond moving forward? My goal became to be great and build a great reputation so that I no longer needed to introduce myself. I figured that with a name like "Demetria," it would not take long.

As I started to have more cases and get into court more often, the condescending behavior from my older male opposing counsel began. You know, the ones who start every conversation with the length of time they have practiced. You know, the kind who appear in court half-prepared but still confident that the case will always go their way in front of a white male judge (most likely a colleague at some point in their career). I learned after several of these experiences that right or wrong, fair or not, I had to be overly prepared and assertive but respectful even when my colleagues were not. I needed to know my cases in and out. Dress the part.

PILLAR 7 - THE COURT EXPERIENCE

Arrive ON TIME. I learned to block out the "I'm better than you" speeches and concentrate on what I was hired to do.

Definitely a balancing act, between believing I was more than competent, overly preparing my cases, and ignoring arrogant and dismissive opposing counsel, all the while keeping in mind that the legal industry continues to be a "good ole boys club," a male, white, "experienced" industry.

Maybe one day this will not be the case, but until that day, this is what we must do. In light of the "Me Too" era and the current unrest we are experiencing as I write this, it is my hope that the times will radically change for those who come after us, but until then, continue to show up and do great work, and you will be known as such.

PREPARING THE CLIENT FOR THE COURT EXPERIENCE.

In addition to preparing yourself for the hearing, you must also prepare your client. This process begins the moment you file your documents or the moment you receive documents from the opposing side. Please remember that most clients have never attended a court appearance before, so it is crucial to explain every step and every procedure. I like to consider us lawyers as "translators" because we translate the legalese to common English for our clients on a daily basis!

Immediately, when we receive a court date, my staff adds the court date to our master calendar and to our management system, and we can also essentially "tag" our client in their court dates and important deadlines. We also include due dates (due dates for the court and due dates we set internally to ensure we do not miss court due dates) and times for the client to speak to me regarding the preparation of their documents and the preparation of the court process, what to wear, not to interrupt (even when the other side has said something untruthful, or when the other side interrupts). In my office, it is mandatory that our clients have a phone conference with me at least 48 hours prior to their hearing or any other important date to ensure the client has an opportunity to ask any questions prior to the court date, knows how to present to the court, and, of course, knows what to wear. The more you can provide your client with the pertinent information for their case, the more your client will feel that their case matters to you.

PILLAR 7

1. *What do I need to prepare for my first court experience?*

2. *Am I familiar with my judicial officer?*

3. *How will I respond to any negativity that may arise?*

4. *Have I prepared my client for what to expect at the hearing?*

PILLAR 8
The Infamous "Work/Life Balance": What Is That?

We always hear about "work/life balance" and the need to strive for work/life balance. As women, we especially worry about showing up and doing our best in our careers and showing up and being the best at home, making sure we are being great wives, raising great children, caring for aging parents, and being the best friends we can be in addition to our many commitments.

I now believe that the notion of work/life balance is unattainable and unfair. Honestly, on any given day, your focus and your priorities can and will change. When building a practice (especially in the early years), there may be months when you are required to prioritize the business, which may take the front seat. Once you begin to establish yourself, your focus may and will change to other priorities.

The beauty of law firm ownership is that you design your days to match your schedule and priorities. For a long period of time, my top priority was my business, until I had my son. For the first time since I opened my practice, my priorities shifted. It was an adjustment, but I found a way to give most of my time to my son while managing the business. Once my son began daycare, I was able to turn up the focus on the business, not in the way that I once did, but a way that was manageable to me at the time.

I encourage you to shift the narrative from work/life balance and not attempt to "balance" too much. Be okay with shifting priorities and give yourself space to accept your shifting responsibilities. I believe it was Oprah who said, "We can have it all, but maybe not all at the same time."

Self-Care. Self-care is KEY. When you fail to take care of yourself, you will burn out extremely fast and not really have what it takes to fully show up for others. The work will always be there, and breaks are extremely important. You know the saying, "It is hard to pour from an empty cup." You want to take the necessary time to replenish your energy as often as necessary to continue the important work that you do and to manage everything you need to do on a daily basis. Identify a self-care routine early on and decide to do something just for yourself as often as you need to do so.

For me, that includes an early morning spiritual practice of meditation, prayer, journaling, and a Peloton ride and/or workout with my personal trainer (Hey, Rick!). I love the peace and beauty of an early morning, so I get up very early, 5:30-ish, to enjoy some time before my son wakes up and to complete my morning practice, which grounds me for the day to come. My self-care also includes an afternoon to myself, mostly Sundays, and I enjoy a nice facial, a nice

PILLAR 8 - THE INFAMOUS "WORK-LIFE BALANCE"

bath, a glass of wine, and a nice book. I try to unplug for as long as I can to simply focus on myself and do what I enjoy. Nothing fancy, just a couple of hours pampering myself. Prior to the COVID-19 pandemic, I also LOVED the spa, and I hope to get back one day, but until then, I will take my early mornings and afternoons. Do not ignore what is necessary for your self-care and well-being, the work will be there.

Extended Breaks. In addition to self-care, the beauty of being the boss is that you can arrange your schedule, which includes VACATIONS for personal breaks, your children's activities, your husband's needs, etc. Your breaks may be limited in the beginning because you are building your practice, but within a few years, you will have more flexibility, and you will know the culture of your business and the best time to take time off, etc. At the beginning of the year, I sit down and block out time: normally, I try to include my son's winter break, spring break, and time in the summer when he is out of school because I do not want to be as busy as I am during the rest of the year. I then inform my staff of my "black-out" dates, which we add to the master calendar, and when our documents are filed, etc., we request that the court clerk not set hearings on those days. Of course, there are times when we still have hearings on those days, or we receive a file with a previously scheduled hearing, but the strategy still works well for my office.

Family. Do not neglect your family. The work will ALWAYS be there. Yes, there may be times when you are required to work late, prepare for important meetings, court hearings, etc., but do not make this the focal point of your life for the rest of your life. The point of having your own practice is to create the life that you want and to show up for what is important for your family.

Enjoy Your Life. Do not save anything for "later." If you want to date, date. If you want to travel for a year, do that. If you want to perform in a local play and take a break, do that. If you want to run the PTA and be a team parent for your children's activities, do that. Life will not stop because you decided to start a business, and yes, it will be important to you, but do not allow the rest of your life to suffer. If you delay your life, you may find yourself, several years later, regretting the chances outside of your practice that you did not take. The goal is to always prioritize what is most important to you and shift accordingly.

PILLAR 8

1. *What are my priorities?*

2. *What is my self-care routine?*

3. *How will I continue to enjoy my life?*

PILLAR 9

If I Knew Then What I Know Now

I made so many mistakes in my fifteen years of practice, some preventable, some part of the "practice of law." I truly hope that you will avoid some of those mistakes by reading this book. I hope you incorporate the principles I have shared for yourself personally and for your business professionally to make sure you are great because we all want to be great.

To date, here are some of the biggest lessons I have learned:

1. **You are running a business AND managing a law firm.** You will not be able to manage a firm without running the business. Do not ignore the business to run the firm, and do not neglect the firm to run the business.

2. **Do not neglect your family or your other life desires.** The work will always be there. The kids' "firsts" of anything will not. Whatever it is—relationship, vacation, new experience—do not save it for "later."

3. **Systems.** You want to run the business; you do not want the business to run you!

4. **Do not sweat the small stuff.** Other attorneys, judges, and clients may be dismissive, unprofessional, and rude, and their response to your skills most of the time has nothing to do with you. Their attitude is not your issue, but their own. If you start responding to everyone who is rude, you are then thrown off your game. Yes, you may sometimes have to draw the line if someone goes too far, but that is rare. Always remain classy and remind yourself that it is not your problem. I sometimes have to silently remind myself, "It is not my business to worry about what others think about me." If you begin to internalize others' behavior, you will be more stressed out than the individual exhibiting the negative behavior.

5. **Preparation, preparation, preparation.** This always works in my favor because people often underestimate me because I am a woman, a black woman. Because of the false assumption that I am inferior because of who I am, I am always prepared and thoroughly review and know my cases. Know your case, know the facts of the case, know the law, and most importantly, know the judge. Preparation also encompasses dressing the part, speaking the part, and being professional to the court and to your opposing counsel, even if they don't deserve it.

6. **Keep your expenses LOW!** Yes, I am mentioning this again. The goal is to earn money, not spend more money than necessary. You also want to be able to cover your expenses in the event you face an emergency or have

low-earning months. You want to also continue to grow your practice, grow your reserves, and, ultimately, build a legacy.

7. **Know the law.** The law is always changing. So it is important to stay on top of the law in your area, especially the major changes. Luckily, most bar organizations host programs to provide you the major changes to the law in your practice area(s). Some attorneys form study groups with their colleagues to also discuss different case scenarios. There is nothing worse than going to court and presenting your case based on bad law. I have seen this happen. It does not matter how long you have been in practice—the law is forever changing.

8. **Be excellent.** You want to be in the driver's seat. Do not play defense—you want to drive the case at the speed that you want and not let opposing counsel steer the case. This means you are on top of your deadlines, file your documents on time, etc. When the case is going at your speed, you know what to expect, what is to come, and how to navigate the case at your rate of speed.

9. **Become an expert.** In many states, lawyers are prohibited from calling themselves "experts" in their respective practice areas without becoming an "expert" or "specialist" through the State Bar process. In California, to become a "certified specialist," you are required to take a one-day exam in your specified practice area and submit an application very similar to the moral character application and additional questions regarding your expertise. Why do this you may ask? For starters, you want to always strive to be the very best that you can be.

It shows your commitment to your practice area, and if you are in a litigation process, it shows the judges that you are at the top of your field. Just an extra bonus to add something to your brand.

10. **If you do not know, ask!** It is called the "practice" of law for a reason. As long as you are in this profession, you will always be learning, and at different stages in your career, you will come across a legal issue that is unfamiliar to you. Form a network of other attorneys in your practice area that you trust, and when the hard stuff comes up, you have a trusted group with whom to discuss your legal issues.

11. **You can do this!** You must believe that you can do this. Family, friends, college roommates, opposing counsel, and everyone in between may tell you a thousand reasons why you "can't." But their limiting beliefs should not concern you. If you have done the work and truly considered your decision and walked through your plan, GO FOR IT. I am here to tell you, YOU CAN DO THIS. You have read enough of this book to know that if I can do it, so can you.

12. **Always treat others how you want to be treated.** As you continue to climb the ladder of success, treat other attorneys, court staff, judges, etc. as you would want to be treated. I have learned that a smile can go a long way, and you never know what someone is going through behind closed doors. You also have no clue when you might see your colleagues again in your career, maybe as a judge in front of whom you may have to appear,

a supervisor, or someone who may be in a position to assist you later. It pays to be kind.

13. **Find a great mentor.** There is wisdom in experience. Find someone in your field who is more experienced and willing to be a listening ear when you face challenges on your journey, who can answer your questions and just simply be there. We all had to start somewhere on our journey, and it is ok to want support and to continue to learn. I know I still love my mentors and call on those more experienced when I get in a jam. One of my very first mentors, Portasha, was everything that I wanted to be as a lawyer, graceful, patient (still working on that), smart, and always well dressed and professional. Her mentorship continues to guide me today as I remember all of the lessons I learned from her, some spoken and some unspoken. Mentors are a godsend!

There is definitely no "right" or "wrong" way to start your practice. If this is truly something you want to do, then DO IT. Also, you will read in the next section that there is no right or wrong way to practice. Everyone is different. Everyone started in different ways, and everyone's journey is different. I wanted you to hear from other amazing women attorneys who bravely went out on their own and happen to be extremely successful.

PILLAR 9

How will I implement the above lessons for my firm's success?

PILLAR 10
It Takes a Village

Each attorney featured here had the courage to take the leap of faith and open her law firm and has managed to make it work every day. I truly admire each attorney mentioned here, and I am always inspired by other women doing what they need to do to keep following their dreams.

In addition to my admiration for each attorney, I wanted you to see that there are varying ways to manage your practice and show you that there is no right way to do so. As you will see below, some have partners, some are solo, there are varying practice areas, etc. Even if you try your firm for some time and decide it is not for you, that is okay too, as you will read below.

It is so comforting to know that there are now many women out there successfully managing their own firms, and you can do the same. What is different now from when most of us began our firms is that you have a village!

After each interview, you can read the biography of each business owner to learn more about the practice area and how to contact the business owner as part of your village, part of your homework to interview others, and, most importantly, to learn. ENJOY!

INTERVIEW 1
ESTEEMED ATTORNEY AND CERTIFIED FAMILY LAW SPECIALIST, ARELIS HUGHES

When did you start thinking about having your own practice?

I started thinking about it a few years after graduating law school, but I decided to wait until I thought the timing was right to venture out on my own. I eventually decided to take a chance in 2018.

Why did you decide 2018 was the right time?

There were changes going on at my firm at the time. I was confident in the amount of legal experience and trial practice I had under my belt. Importantly, my children were older. When you open a new business, it becomes your newborn baby. You have to have the energy and time to invest in it. In 2018, everything lined up and pointed me in the direction of embarking on my own business.

I always knew at some point I would have my own law firm. I grew up in a family of entrepreneurs, and my husband is an entrepreneur. It was just a matter of time before I started my own law practice. I wanted to have the right amount of legal experience so that I felt comfortable advocating for people without the safety net of a large firm behind me. After completing years of continuing education and handling trials on my own, I felt my knowledge base was more than sufficient. I had operated my own non-legal business

PILLAR 10 - IT TAKES A VILLAGE

previously and was already familiar with the management aspect. The newness was putting the practice of law and the management of a business together. The timing was just perfect in 2018 for me to branch out and start this venture.

What were some of your fears when deciding to open your own firm?

Definitely the fluctuation of income. Being fully responsible for my income as well as income for any future employees was a concern. On the flip side, being able to control my own income was a driving force as well. Another concern was balancing the duties associated with the business and administrative side with the duties associated with the legal side. I was uncertain how to adjust from being just a practicing attorney whose only focus was supervising my caseload to being both a practicing attorney and a business manager. I would now be responsible for supervising my caseload while meeting the demands of a growing Family Law practice.

I was quickly reminded that starting a new business was like having a baby. There is an increase of time demands and commitments. However, that fear was alleviated because I knew having my own business would allow me the flexibility with my schedule to do tasks on my own time.

How did you manage your family life with having a new practice?

It has definitely been a challenge. But the perks outweigh the hurdles. A new law practice needs your attention, and other responsibilities end up taking a back seat. This was a main reason why I waited until my children were older. My children still need me but are a bit more independent, so I was able to devote the time I needed to start my practice. The flexibility of having my own firm allowed me to do that.

Sometimes it means that you are going to have long nights, just like you would if you had a newborn. You get to decide when to work and when to spend time with your family as well. It has been a blessing to be able to attend my children's functions without the fear of missing work because I am able to attend to my work commitments on my time.

Now you also have a partner. Correct?

Yes.

What is it like having a partner?

I think it's the best decision that I've made in business. I owned a business prior to owning my law practice. I know what it's like to do it on my own, and I know what it's like to do it with someone else. My business partner and I call each other Yin and Yang because we are the perfect blend together. Her weaknesses are my strengths, and my weaknesses are her strengths. For instance, I enjoy going to court, attending depositions, and handling settlement conferences, while she enjoys doing case analysis, legal research, and writing. We share the responsibility of managing the practice together. It is the perfect match.

What is your advice for anyone considering solo practice vs. partnership?

It is important to have someone who has common goals and common beliefs. It's funny because my partner and I finish each other's sentences and often say we have the same brain.

PILLAR 10 – IT TAKES A VILLAGE

We may say it differently, but the bottom line is, we think the same way. We have the same belief system when it comes to our goals for our clients. For example, clients will send us questions and, without knowing that one has already responded, we respond with exactly the same advice.

Your partner should be someone that you fully trust and can mesh with. It is important to find the right blend, and I will be honest, the right partner is difficult to find. If you're lucky enough like I was to be able to find the ideal partner, I wouldn't pass up that opportunity.

What advice would you give to a woman who is struggling to decide how to open her own law practice and manage her own life?

I think you need to do a lot of self-reflection. Prayer and meditation helped me. You need to know yourself and your personality and look internally for what will be the right time for you. The right time is going to be different for everyone. I have friends who were ready to start their own practice immediately after passing the bar. That wasn't for me, and I knew I needed to take a different road. I wanted to work for a big firm. I wanted to gain the knowledge and training from working for experienced attorneys. My partner and I have been doing this for a long time. We met at a large firm and grew our knowledge and practice base together.

Working at a firm allowed me to handle cases on my own, meet judges, gain experience, and develop my professional reputation without having to deal with the administrative and marketing aspects. By the time I opened my own firm, I felt really solid about my legal ability. The business aspect of operating a firm takes time. You do not just get to be a lawyer—you also have to run the business. You need to be prepared for the energy that it takes. You have to be able to find that perfect point of balance for you, and only you will know when that right time is. Nobody can tell you when the right time is for you.

Do you believe your experience is any different because you are a minority woman?

I primarily practice in Orange County, which is a predominantly white environment. I have utilized the fact that people may underestimate me not only because I am a minority woman, but because I look young. I often surprise my opponents who have not had a case with me before.

I'm sure others misjudge me due to the color of my skin or because I am a woman. It is definitely likely that I have not been hired due to one of those things, and that is okay. Clearly that was not a client I was meant to have.

I've been able to establish a positive reputation in the legal community, and I take that very seriously. Preparation, honesty, and credibility are key. I strive for people to notice those things about me versus how I look. I think attorneys that have worked with me in the past that may have first only noticed my appearance, now say that I am well-prepared, honest, and a force to be reckoned with.

If you knew then what you know now, how would your law experience be different?

Formulate your knowledge base in the area you intend to practice, and then go out there and try it. Argue the motions, take the depositions, handle the trials. Judges can be forgiving when you are new, and they know you are going to

PILLAR 10 – IT TAKES A VILLAGE

make mistakes. Learn from those mistakes. If you prepare in advance and walk into a courtroom knowing your file from top to bottom, the experience you will get is like no other. Take the opportunity to watch top-notch attorneys put on a hearing or read a transcript from one of those hearings. Look at the way they ask questions, how they follow-up, and assess their cross-examination style. Then try out what will work for you. That's how you learn. You learn from doing.

You must also enjoy helping people. If it's your desire to help people, you will never go wrong. It's not about making money. It's about the service that we provide to others.

Arelis Hughes' Bio:

Arelis Hughes is a Founding Partner at Cooper Hughes, an accomplished Family Law firm in Orange, California. As a Certified Specialist in Family Law, Arelis zealously and passionately advocates for her clients in negotiations, court proceedings, and trials. She represents clients in a wide variety of Family Law cases involving child custody, child support, spousal support, property identification and division, reimbursements, domestic violence, and termination of parental rights. Her practice is dedicated exclusively to Family Law matters in Southern California.

Arelis is a respected litigator and negotiator. She is a graduate of the American Bar Association Family Law Trial Advocacy Institute. Arelis has thrived in her legal career for over 20 years. She began her legal career as a paralegal, which allows her a unique perspective of the nuances of legal practice. Arelis then attended Loyola Law School and immediately began practicing Family Law upon her graduation. Arelis can be reached at 949.284.4200 and info@cooperhugheslaw.com.

INTERVIEW 2
ESTEEMED WILLS AND ESTATES ATTORNEY, ESTHER HOPKINS

When did you decide to open your own law practice?

I first jumped out on my own in 2005, after practicing for 13 years with firms. I was working as an employee at a 100 lawyer firm when I decided to start my own practice. I first started my own practice with another lawyer that I was working with at the time. I started a partnership at first, I think more than anything, because I was afraid to go out by myself, to be honest. However, we were located in different parts of the county. He was down in Torrance, and I in the Conejo Valley (approximately 35 miles away from each other). After we got started, I realized that the partnership did not make sense. One, we both had different ideas regarding the type of work we wanted to do. And number two, we were far from each other from a location standpoint. We were not really doing anything to help each other. Because we were distant in proximity, we actually doubled our costs instead of sharing our costs. So we agreed to dissolve our partnership. My current permutation of the practice was opened in October 2008. This was right before the recession.

Why did you decide to go out on your own?

I hated civil litigation. That's what I was doing before I went out on my own. Hated it. I knew that I had to change

PILLAR 10 - IT TAKES A VILLAGE

something. I wanted to find an area of law that was more appealing to me. I happened to do an MCLE class with a lot of credits because I was behind on credits, and my deadline for reporting was fast approaching. I took an estate planning MCLE course because it had a lot of credits, and that was it. After going through the course, I said, this is what I want to do. And so I was either going to quit the practice of law altogether, or I was going to quit and practice another area of law and be on my own. Ultimately, I just quit my job and pulled the band-aid off and started practicing a whole new other area of law. I first started a practice with a partner in 2005, and then I opened my own solo firm in 2008.

Did you and your partner have a transition plan or any plan when you left the firm?

There was some planning. My partner wanted to be transactional business, and I wanted to do estate planning and transactional business. At the time, that was our vision. However, because we were new to our law practice, my partner and I knew that we would have to continue doing some litigation until we developed new business. But we just kept getting pulled more and more into litigation. Because the litigation business paid our bills, I was not putting in the effort to grow the estate planning practice. Our thought was to take what we could so that we could take care of the overhead and expenses. So there was a plan, but it wasn't as concrete as you would think. We figured out what our practice areas would be. We figured who our clients were going to be. We developed operating systems like filing, organization, and billing. But it was just the two of us at first, so it was not overcomplicated. We just kept building and perfecting our systems over time. We created a budget.

What are the pros and cons of having a partner?

The first partner I had in the very beginning, he was great. I loved him. And I will tell you, we really were a good team. If we were geographically located in the same place, I think it would have worked out. Having a partner makes good sense if you have the right partner. Partners can share costs, and you can rely on each other to brainstorm on legal and business issues. But for us, it didn't make any sense.

Moving forward, I did have another partner. This partner was geographically close to me. The benefits were that we shared employees, shared space, and shared costs, and we could collaborate. However, if you do not have the right person, none of those benefits really matter. It will not work if you do not have the same vision for what the practice should be. So, yes, I think there's a lot of benefit to having a partner if you have the right partner. I just think that we as lawyers do better when we can collaborate with others. The con is that you could end up with the wrong partner. That is the hardest part to figure out.

What was your major fear going from big firm law practice to owning your own law practice?

The loss of a steady paycheck! How am I going to pay my bills? That was a huge fear. I also went out and started practicing a completely different area of law. So there was a little bit of fear that I'm going to go out and market myself for this new area of law, and I'm new at it this area of law. Also, it's one thing to market an established law firm, but it's another

PILLAR 10 - IT TAKES A VILLAGE

thing to market yourself. From a personality standpoint, that was hard for me. I had to get out of my comfort zone and learn to ask people to trust me. It was easy to say trust us, not trust me. And getting out there and selling yourself, it is a hard thing. You have to have a certain personality to feel okay marketing yourself and tooting your own horn, I guess. That is an uncomfortable place for me.

Did you think about what it meant to be a woman in solo practice?

That's been an issue through my entire legal career. I felt it when I walked into a deposition and the male opposing attorney asked me if I was the court reporter and when another male attorney called me "Little Miss." So that was already there. When I acquired my practice, certain male referral professionals would form boys' clubs and only referred complex and sophisticated matters to men. I had a financial advisor tell my networking group that I handled simple estate planning matters and the male in our group handled the complex matters. The reality was that the male attorney was practicing for less time than I had been practicing, and he would often call me for legal advice. At no time did I ever communicate to anyone that I only wanted to handle simple matters.

As a result, I often felt that I had to neutralize the perception that I am a female attorney and a female practice. I would never discuss any motherly obligations or obligations that were "female" for fear that I would not be taken seriously. I always had to work harder to prove myself than the men in the room did.

Being a minority woman, I think there is an added layer of pressure. You must prove yourself more. You cannot for one second show a chink in the armor.

I think we as women have to stop and just be ourselves. And stop apologizing. We have to stop apologizing for who we are and how we are and stop trying to assimilate to the boys' club. We work to assimilate in their club. Well, how about if we create our own inclusive club and do business our way? Unfortunately, there aren't enough women out there doing that. Most just try to fit into the old model.

What do you wish you knew then that you know now?

Don't be afraid to ask for what you want from the marketing perspective. Ask people to send you referrals. Don't just give a spiel about what you do. Remember to do the asking. Take that extra leap and say, "Think about me when you have clients." I also think every new business owner should take a course in sales. You have to because becoming a salesperson is vital to the survival of your business.

Number two, from the business perspective, definitely plan. Get a business plan. What are my expenses definitely going to be? Do not forget to add in what is the minimum amount you need from a financial standpoint to survive and to make this venture worth your time. That expense must be included and is non-negotiable. If you cannot keep to this number, then this venture is not worth it.

Once you determine the expenses, you must ask yourself, what is the number of matters or hours I must have to cover this expense? This is hugely important. You need to know those numbers.

PILLAR 10 - IT TAKES A VILLAGE

Do not take crappy clients. Stay away from these clients. They will waste your time. Time that you could be spending marketing and getting good clients. Do not be afraid to say no. And it is okay to reject people because they will suck your time and take away from you growing your business. That took me a while to figure out for sure. Do not waste your time with people who refuse to provide you with your requested retainer. You must take money up front and do not be shy about it.

And if they give you a hard time, then say no. Absolutely say no. If they are not willing to pay for your retainer up front, do not waste your time because they're going to give you a hard time every step of the way. And you do not work for free.

Any advice for women specifically?

At the end of the day, you want to have more control of your life because that is definitely not what I had when I was working in a firm. You control your destiny versus someone else.

However, don't think that you are just going to go out and practice law. It takes a very different kind of personality to operate your own practice because you will now be managing a business. You will now need to market and become a salesperson. You may now have to manage employees. So you have to understand that you are not just going to hang a shingle. There are so many other things that go into operating a practice besides practicing law.

Finally, do not change who you are as a women's practice. Ignore the noise from the boys' clubs. Run your practice your way. Surround yourself with men and women who support your vision for your woman-owned practice.

Esther Hopkins' Bio:

Esther Hopkins, founder and principal of the Law Offices of Esther Hopkins, P.C., provides personalized legal counsel to individuals and families in the areas of estate planning, business succession planning, probate and trust administration, and special needs planning. She is particularly adept at handling the planning and administration challenges unique to high-net-worth individuals and families, complex estates, and business.

Esther received her B.A. in Political Science from the University of California at Los Angeles in 1990. She earned her Juris Doctor from Loyola Law School, Los Angeles, in 1993. She became a member of the State Bar of California in 1993. In addition, Esther is fluent in Spanish.

INTERVIEW 3
ESTEEMED CRIMINAL DEFENSE ATTORNEY, JILL CARTER

Why did you decide to open your own law practice?

About midway through law school, I questioned if I wanted to be a practicing attorney, but I continued my education. I graduated in 2004 and took the bar. Thank God, I passed that first time because I probably did not have enough interest at the time to take it again. I took it in California, but then I went back to Houston, which is where I went to law school. While there, I did not practice law, I continued doing real estate investing which I started during law school.

A big part of why I lost interest in law midway through law school was that I started getting into real estate investing. That experience is one of the things that drew me to entrepreneurship.

As I continued to consider my next steps, I really thought having my own practice would be a way to kill two birds with one stone, honestly.

So, that is what I did.

Tell us about your journey.

When I returned from Houston in the summer of 2005, I worked at a small law firm for about four months to learn the ins and outs of running a private practice. I knew I wanted to have my own practice, but I did not know the first thing about operating a law practice.

I was trying to learn a craft and learn more about law firm management at the same time. I do not know if I would recommend starting a practice without working for someone for at least a short period of time.

When I started at the firm, I wanted to learn everything possible about my craft and about the practice. I started to consider how I would manage my firm. Some practices I learned I liked and some I did not, but if I did not have the experience, I would not know how to select what I really liked and what I did not.

During this time, I was open to networking opportunities, several organizations, and anything I could get my hands on to just get out there and get involved. I had to make sure my colleagues knew who I was, and I wanted to learn more about my colleagues in my practice area.

I also was not afraid to study good attorneys and often arranged meetings so I could ask my many questions. I built a really strong network of people that I could text or call from court or run out in the hall and call because I spent a lot of time getting to know people and letting them know what I was trying to do. And that was probably the smartest thing I did.

As new law firm owners, how can we strengthen our court presence if we did not go to court much in previous firms?

I never appeared in court on my own when I worked for the firm. So, when I first started my own practice, I was mostly doing appearances for attorneys I met and handling continuances and quite simple matters.

I was still very nervous. I would arrive when the doors opened and try to talk to the clerk to attempt to ease my fears. I would tell the clerk, "I'm new, I really don't know what to say. I am here, but I'm not ready. I just want to listen to a few people first." Most courts understood and let me watch. I would watch other attorneys, handle my matter, and after, I might sit there all day, even into the afternoon, and just listen to experienced attorneys speak to the judge, learn what to say, how to present to the court, and whatever else I could learn.

After six months of doing general appearances, I started feeling more comfortable and informed attorneys I made

PILLAR 10 - IT TAKES A VILLAGE

appearances for that I was ready to handle more complicated cases. There were times when the DA wanted to negotiate the cases with me, and I would have to run and text the attorney like, well, hey, I can work something out, and most attorneys would give me the authority to try to work out the case.

To build court confidence, go sit in courtrooms and just listen to what is on calendar. Listen to what is going on. What are people saying? What are some common things that you hear? For instance, when I first started going to court, I did not know what a preliminary hearing was. So, eventually I am like, okay, what is a preliminary hearing? Then I would go and hear how attorneys handled preliminary hearings. I did the same thing with trials; I'd highly advise new attorneys to watch trials in your practice area from start to finish.

After I was more comfortable with court procedure and being in court, I started to sit second chair on trials, so I was then actively learning the skills necessary to do trials. Eventually, I started to cross-examine witnesses and do an opening or a closing, and the first chair attorneys would then give me feedback before I really went out on my own.

So, fortunately, by the time I did my first jury trial by myself, I probably sat through four trials at counsel tables as second chair for other attorneys—FOR FREE—but the experience was priceless, and I felt very prepared when I started handling trials on my own. In the early stages, I was truly fortunate to handle trials in front of a judge who was patient and willing to give me feedback at the end of my trials. I also felt like his courtroom was a learning courtroom, which was extremely helpful. Because of that experience, I felt extremely comfortable handling trials in other places.

My relationships with more seasoned criminal attorneys are invaluable especially earlier on in my career. First, I was provided opportunities to learn, and then they became resources and references for me when I had questions.

How do you "balance" your practice, your family, and other relationships?

Structure. In Criminal Law, most of my court appearances occur between 9:00 a.m. and 12:00 p.m. every day. After lunch, for the most part, I am done with court. I then plan the rest of my day around my family and other responsibilities.

When I first started my practice, I had a young daughter and was still learning how to structure my day to properly tackle everything I needed to do. I remember I had a murder case, and my daughter was about four or five, and she walked by with an autopsy picture of a dead person's torso at the coroner's office and started counting all the punctures from the stab wounds (they were numbered). Luckily, at the time, she did not really understand what it was. Thank God, it did not traumatize her. But it just really got me in the mindset of separating my work responsibilities from my home responsibilities and of separating my work time from my home time. And that might mean when she goes to bed, I began working again.

When I got married, my husband was also adamant about me limiting my clients' access to my time. He asked me, "Do you feel like all lawyers are this accessible?" That really stuck with me. When I considered some of the attorneys I knew and respected the most, the vast majority of them set limits on their time and accessibility. I had to draw a similar line. I

PILLAR 10 – IT TAKES A VILLAGE

never thought about it that way, but he was right. In the early days, I made myself entirely too open and available.

Even now with both of my daughters, I know that most days I am unable to do much at their schools before noon; but I can be there once a week in the afternoon. I remember when my first daughter was in kindergarten, I was in that classroom all the time, while at the same time, building my practice. I always remember how confident she was seeing me come into her class—she knew she could count on me being there. And that was such a great moment for both of us.

So fast forward to now, I do not have a standing time to volunteer anymore, but I always arrange my schedule to volunteer for every field trip or big event at their school. Both of them are my priority, and I feel like I'm at a point where if I know something's coming up, and my older daughter has a volleyball game, or my younger daughter needs to go to the dentist at a time when I'm normally in court, I just make sure I plan ahead and structure my days around their needs.

There are times when the judge wants you back on certain days, and earlier in my career, I would often acquiesce to whatever the court wanted me to do. Over the years, when I got more comfortable, I began to be firm about picking the days that did not interfere with my family responsibilities as often as I could.

What other jewels can you share with us?

Be a serious stickler about your calendaring and making sure that you calendar all of your court dates, preferably in two places. You do not want to lose the court's respect and have clerks calling you in your absence. If you are going to be late, please call ahead and inform the clerk, so they know you are respecting their time and their calendar.

Often, I can cover three courts in one day. Once I plan my day and know where I will attend first, I will then call the other courts well in advance to inform the clerks of my other appearances and provide my ETA and my contact number.
I remember one time this judge said, "Miss Carter, you are a real class act." He told me that he could not remember the last time an attorney called to say they would arrive at 9:15. Lawyers typically do not call unless they will be a couple hours late or so, but I wanted to set myself apart from others as someone who did her best to be where I said I was going to be.

In the beginning, find ways to set yourself apart from what lawyers typically do. You want the courts to know that you are serious and professional, especially if you work for yourself. In solo practice, you can't ride off the reputation of your office or your colleagues, so you are setting the standards for yourself. It's important to develop good habits early on.

It is also important to have interests outside of your work. I cannot emphasize enough how having hobbies and interests has kept me grounded and balanced. My main interest has been travel, so much so that I created a successful travel blog that has been a passion project for me for the last couple of years.

It is crucial to find means of self-care and really make time for them. The stress from this career can LITERALLY KILL YOU. We are hired to solve people's problems, and this is often true no matter what area of law you practice.

PILLAR 10 - IT TAKES A VILLAGE

That means we are often immersed in people's lowest and toughest moments that they will face. We take on their stress and anxiety. Even though we are not always affected by it, we are often shouldering many stressful cases at once and may not always notice the impact that stress has on us. Our clients rely on us to improve their situations and create good outcomes for them. That work can drain all your energy if you let it. You cannot pour from an empty cup. It does not serve you or your clients. There is not a reward for the most overworked attorney or the lawyer who pulls the most all-nighters or exists on coffee alone.

PRESERVE AND PROTECT YOUR PEACE AT ALL COSTS, SIS. Self-care and rest are a must! Accordingly, we need to make time for activities that are stress relievers. For me, that has been traveling and writing. Two things that I love, in fact love so much that I'm transitioning out of law to focus more on these two things that I've grown very passionate about.

I love this interview because you are currently transitioning out of your practice. Can you tell us why you are transitioning to another interest instead of maintaining your practice and following your new passion?

I have thoroughly enjoyed my time as a criminal defense attorney in private practice. I have learned so much, and I know I've made a positive impact on my clients' lives. But recently, especially as my kids get older and their needs change, I've begun putting a plan together for a smooth transition to a less demanding schedule. This has been a time-consuming process that involved gradually taking less and less cases and then limiting my practice to less serious cases. As I've been preparing for this transition, I've discovered that an added benefit is having more time to concentrate on the things that I'm most passionate about but often get pushed to the back burner because of the demands of my career.

Traveling and writing have always been hobbies and passions of mine, but now I will be able to pursue those areas more aggressively. I will be able to devote more time to my travel blog and business services like group travel, products, and writing opportunities. It'll be nice to travel and not pull up files to review while sitting in a cafe or pool/beach side. Fifteen years in, I think the time is right.

I will still practice, but on a much smaller and more selective scale. I will always be passionate about issues surrounding Criminal Law, specifically as it relates to black and brown people. But I am excited to pursue other interests by taking this huge step. The lessons I have learned as a criminal defense attorney in private practice will last a lifetime.

Jill Carter's Bio:

Jill Carter has been a criminal defense attorney in private practice for the last 15 years. In that time, she's represented countless clients throughout Southern California. Jill is also a wife and mother to two girls, ages 12 and 4. When she's not practicing, you can find her traveling, writing about her travels in her travel blog, or dreaming about/planning her next trip.

INTERVIEW 4
ESTEEMED ATTORNEY AND FAMILY LAW SPECIALIST, LEENA HINGNIKAR

When and why did you start your own practice?

I started in July of 2019 because I wanted something of my own; I wanted to learn the ins and outs of starting a business in addition to practicing law. I also wanted to test my own legal skills and figure out what I was capable of doing on my own without having a powerhouse type of firm to back me up. And, I mean, we all have experiences with firms, politics, salaries, and all the things that come along with having the firm structure, and I did not want to deal with all that anymore. I wanted the independence of being able to decide all of that for myself.

How long were you practicing before you went out on your own?

Eleven to twelve years.

What were your major fears when you considered having your own practice?

I think all women suffer from some type of imposter syndrome, and you would think that after practicing for 11 or 12 years, you would feel completely solid to be able to practice law on your own. But when you are with a firm, as helpful as it is and as wonderful as it is, it also sort of handicaps you into relying on others, always having help and people to bounce ideas off of. And I think it kind of helps to cultivate that imposter syndrome because you are always scared to do it on your own without the help of all these smart people.

Another major fear was will the clients come? What sets me apart from every other Family Law attorney who is a solo practitioner in Los Angeles? There are so many of us, so why would a client choose me over somebody else? And how would they even know about me?

I think to some level I still have that imposter syndrome. A lot of days, I wake up and tell myself I can do this, I am not an imposter, I know what I am doing. The clients came, and I still wonder if they are going to be here tomorrow or the day after, if I will get new ones, and if I will keep getting referrals. What I realized is that these fears never leave, you just learn to manage them once you realize your practice is up and running. You take leaps of faith every day waiting for that phone to ring and that new client to call. Running a practice is cyclical, and you have to be okay with that. Some weeks you will be very busy, and other times, you won't be.

Did you create a plan when you left your previous firm?

I took a very long time to decide I was leaving my prior firm, but I didn't have a plan as to what I was going to do. I had the luxury of giving the firm over two months' notice before I left. During that two months, I set things up for myself. I set up an S Corp, I opened up my business bank accounts, set up QuickBooks, got all of my form files ready (like retainer agreements and the like), and worked on setting up a really basic website. My website was not finished until after I left. I wish I had been one of those people who had everything set up, with logos and office space and all those types of things, but I was the person winging it. And I remember that I kept asking you questions every time I hit a stop and did not know the answer to a question. I did not even know where to open my business bank accounts.

I think I was lucky because after having been with the firm so long, I had met so many friends who are solos, so just being in the industry, I had a lot of people to ask for advice. I mean, I do not know that that is always available when you are an attorney and you go out on your own, but I had tons of resources. My old firm basically let me take everything, like said to me do not reinvent the wheel: take all of our forms, take all of our retainer agreements, we have gone through all this before, we want you to be successful. In that way, I was super lucky.

A lot of women (and I emphasize women because that is who I am writing the book for) are really afraid to just take the leap. So now that you have done it and pretty recently, what are three things you would say to someone thinking about law firm ownership?

I would say, first off, we all have imposter syndrome and at some level think we cannot do it but that should not prevent you from actually doing it. So I think that that is really important to know because everybody thinks it is really individual to them, and they just have kind of this insecurity about whatever it is they want to do, but it is not. I think most people have it at some level but that does not mean that you will not be successful.

I think the second thing people told me is that the clients will come. I mean every solo I talked to said exactly the same thing. You do not have a website, do not worry, the clients will come. You do not have everything you want set up, you do not have all the connections, you do not have all the networking relationships, don't worry, the clients will come. And they do. Further, to this point, having that network is a huge key to the success of a firm. I think that because all my clients so far have been solely referral based. I mean it has not come from anywhere else, not my website, not marketing, not anything else I have done. If you have a good network, your firm will get off to the right start.

I think the third most important thing people have to think about is do they want to be their own boss, and is that something they are actually capable of doing. Not everybody wants that lifestyle. You have to be motivated to be a self-starter, and it is a lot of work. You have to bill less to make money, but you also spend a ton of your time doing administrative work, billing work, networking, and all the stuff that others take care of for you when you are at a firm. The positive is that the payoff is all yours. As an added bonus, you can take the type of clients you want to take. You are no longer obligated to represent clients who your old bosses would bring to the firm—you can represent the clients who will respect you. So it is hard work, but you definitely feel more respected.

To sum it all up, I think that it is harder for women in our profession to be respected just like in many other professions. I think that there is definitely an old boys' club in the legal profession, and it is really hard to break into that. Specific to our Family Law universe, the number of minority women practicing Family Law is very small. You have to work harder to prove yourself and to gain respect because

PILLAR 10 – IT TAKES A VILLAGE

it is not automatically given to you. I think that gaining that respect can be more manageable when you are on your own. You are no longer fighting within a firm's structure and the outside universe of lawyers to gain respect—you are only fighting that outside universe of lawyers. It's one less thing to deal with. I think you gain a lot of credibility when you are running your own practice.

What is something or some things you wish you would have known before you got started?

I wish I would have been a little bit more "eyes open" as to how much administrative work goes into running a law practice. I have been learning on the job, and it's definitely taken up a lot of my time. I remember when I was first starting out, figuring out how to use QuickBooks took like full two days. It is just things that you do not necessarily think about, like setting up a website and how long that takes, how long it takes to find software that works for you, etc.

I came into my practice sub-contracting with my old firm. I did work with them on a couple of cases, so I did not bring any clients over with me. I think that if somebody is thinking about leaving and they have the ability to take their book of business/clients with them, that is really important. If you have that book of business, you could really jump start your practice. You will automatically have a stream of income, and you will not have to necessarily start from scratch.

Another tip is that you do not need an office if you are a solo practitioner. If you can work from home and have virtual space to meet clients if necessary, that will save you so much in overheard costs. I think that was one of the best decisions that I made in this first year.

Leena Hingnikar's Bio:

Leena represents a wide range of clients, from stay-at-home parents to business owners, whether the case involves complex courtroom litigation, mediation settlement matters, or even consulting services.

Leena began her career at the preeminent Los Angeles Family Law firm, Walzer Melcher LLP, where she practiced for over ten years and became a partner before deciding to start her own firm.

In addition to her practice, Leena spends time volunteering to further advance the Family Law community. She is currently the Vice-Chair and Live Education Chair of the Family Law Section of the California Lawyers Association.

Leena is a Los Angeles native. She lives in the Los Angeles area with her husband and labradoodle. When she is not practicing law, Leena enjoys traveling abroad, the Hollywood Bowl, and wine tasting.

INTERVIEW 5
ESTEEMED EMPLOYMENT LAW ATTORNEY, MIKA HILARIE

Why did you decide to open your own law practice?

I've always had aspirations of having my name on the door, per se, and it became clear after I gave birth to my third child that having my own practice would afford me the autonomy

PILLAR 10 - IT TAKES A VILLAGE

that I needed to juggle both being a mother and being an attorney. I just felt that being able to allocate my time on any given day towards the things that were important to me under my own terms was the way that I could be successful as both a mother and a lawyer.

How long did you practice before you opened your own firm?

I practiced for approximately four and a half years.

What is your current practice area?

I have primarily practiced in the area of labor and employment. I started off doing defense work for the first four to five years, which I thought was great because I received great training. I now consider myself a civil rights lawyer not just an employment lawyer because I handle civil rights in the workplace, police brutality, and wrongful death cases.

What were your major considerations before opening your doors?

I asked myself: Coming from a defense firm, what makes me, being only out of law school for four years, capable to manage my own firm? Doubt of the unknown or not knowing what you don't know is hard. But there are great ways to make sure that you have support and guidance. When you hang your own shingle, it is a fallacy that you have to go at it alone. When I first opened up my own firm, I developed and cultivated relationships with more senior lawyers. I still do that today. It is also important to join your local bar associations such as Black Women Lawyers Association of Los Angeles, Inc., or Los Angeles Bar Association. I also joined other bar groups and regularly meet with others in my practice area, which is fantastic because most of us are solo practitioners or have small firms. We meet monthly and talk about firm management, cases, etc.

What were the determining factors for you to take the leap of faith and open your firm?

Well, there wasn't one thing. I just remember speaking to another lawyer in my firm, and I told him that I was really thinking about starting my own firm. He was also thinking of going out on his own. We then had the law firm discussion, and it went from there. I went into a very careful planning stage. So it didn't happen overnight. I reached out to other plaintiffs' lawyers that I respected and who I knew would be open to having a dialogue with me. I would invite them to lunch, and I just interviewed them about all aspects of managing a firm and being a civil rights lawyer. I asked tough questions such as, "What are the things that are going to keep me up at night?" So then I developed a road map. I typed out the formal checklist and assigned my partner and me tasks to be completed. As we worked through the list, we decided when the optimal day was to open our doors.

What are three things you wish you knew then that you learned throughout your practice?

Money management. No one likes to face this one because it's hard to look in the mirror and face our flaws. I definitely would have done better with my money if I was a better money manager. Also, when you have your own practice, you don't have certain protections you may have at a bigger law firm. For instance, you have to save money for long-term sickness, medical insurance, vacations, etc. Unless you plan ahead, you can't just up and leave for six weeks. You have to plan out things differently. So I think being a great money manager really bodes well for people to start their own firm. I would suggest taking a course in money management and firm management for better money management practices. There is also a book called Profit First that I would recommend.

The second thing is I would have given myself a little more grace with how long it would have taken me to become, in my eyes, financially successful. Rome was not built in a day—neither will your law firm.

Third, just because you open up your own firm, don't be afraid to ask for help or seek advice. Even now, I will pick up the phone, and I will call lawyers I trust to get other viewpoints. One of the things I love about Johnnie Cochran is that he valued the input from all the lawyers on his team. Create your own brain trust and do not hesitate to reach out to bounce ideas. When you feel supported by your colleagues and other trusted attorneys, you become more confident and feel less stressed.

What are some of the cons of law firm ownership?

Money does not come in on a regular basis, and that is where good money management comes into play. You also have a different kind of stress because everything rests on your shoulders, and at times, it can be overwhelming. Last year, I probably had the worst year of my life. I was used to being a stellar, high-performing individual, and when everything went wrong in my personal life, my professional life was heavily impacted. Unlike at big firms, I did not have anyone to delegate my work to or the ability to just take an extended leave of absence.

What do you love about law firm ownership?

I enjoy being a business owner tremendously. It affords me a great sense of accomplishment and pride. I love that I have created something from the ground up. I've been able to build something that is so rewarding—it's like giving birth to a child, and it can never be taken away from me, and so from a professional standpoint, it's one of the proudest things I've accomplished. Second, I get to decide how I want my name to be, my reputation to be, what type of work I do, who I work with, clients I get to work with. Owning my own firm allows me complete control over my career. Even at a large firm, if you're a partner, you don't always have the same decision-making power. Third, law firm ownership has allowed me the flexibility to raise my four children and be a lawyer on my own terms. I can work at 2 a.m. if I need to so that I can be present at every school function or athletic event for my children. It is very worthwhile for me. I was the room-parent for every single child at least one year. I never missed a sporting event. I also have the opportunity to be a mentor to other African American women, to see "our" names on the "door," big or small. Also, to be a pillar of the African American legal community and beyond is also a pro for me. I also can hire other vendors and be a part of the economic system in hiring African Americans and other young women. I think it is important and impactful.

What advice would you give to women wanting to start their own practice?

Make sure you understand that law firm ownership is a business first. It is also important to know your worth, which is necessary to becoming successful, such as setting your hourly rate and not negotiating down with vendors, etc. A lot of women tend to back down from confrontation. We tend to go along with the "norm" and want to keep things nice. You do not need to be arbitrarily vicious or aggressive, but you have to stand your ground. A lot of men do this all the time without second thought. For women, it doesn't always come as naturally. Confidence is key. This is still the "good old boys' network," so it is important to remain vigilant and keep your own personal mantra, understanding that we are equal and just as qualified, just as confident, if not more. Yes, you will advocate for your clients, but most importantly, you must learn to advocate for yourself and your firm.

Mika Hilaire's Bio:

Mika is a founding partner of the Equal Rights Law Group, focusing on Employment Law and litigation. She earned her Bachelor of Arts degree from the University of California, Berkeley, with a major from the nationally recognized Rhetoric Department. After earning her law degree from the University of California Hastings College of the Law and her admission to The State Bar of California in 2001, Mika began her legal career, immediately focused on Employment Law, giving her almost 20 years of valuable experience in the practice area. She has secured countless successful settlements and verdicts for her clients, including one recent case that resulted in a $47 million verdict. Her long and impressive record of success has led to a number of honors, including a "Superb" rating from Avvo. Mika was recognized as a Southern California Super Lawyer in 2019 and 2020, and as a Southern California Rising Star from 2007-2013, for her representation of clients in Employment Law. She is a regular guest speaker on local, state, and national levels. She is also a member of a number of organizations, including the Los Angeles County Bar Association.

INTERVIEW 6
ESTEEMED ENTERTAINMENT ATTORNEY, NYANZA SHAW

How long did you work for someone else before you decided to go out on your own?

I decided that I wanted to have my own practice before I started practicing law, the goal was always to have my own practice. I worked at a firm in a non-legal role for a year between college and law school because I wanted to learn about how law firms operated. After graduating law school, I had a few firm jobs before I went out on my own after five years of practicing. The last one I had, I was working part-time for the firm and developing my practice at the same time. I have been out on my own officially for 19 years.

How do you feel about attorneys opening their law practices right after law school?

I understand that in this Google era where it is easy to gain information via the internet, some young lawyers are eager to start their practices the day after graduation. I am just not a big proponent of that because I believe new lawyers should

PILLAR 10 - IT TAKES A VILLAGE

have some experience working in a firm and understanding the process of running a firm, the business side of it, before going out on their own. I think it is amazingly easy to look up information, read books, and understand the law, but that is different from the practical application of how running a law firm business actually works in the real world. I would suggest that a new lawyer get at least a couple of years of experience working at a firm before starting their own firm to understand how running a law firm works.

When I worked at a firm during the year between college and law school, I was very intentional about learning everything about how the law firm operated. I was not even there to learn law. I was not even a law student yet, but I made sure that I learned all about the different roles and systems throughout the firm.

Everyone wants to practice in the Entertainment Law space, what is your advice for those who believe entertainment is the only way to go?

First, you should have an idea of the different roles that exist, the different practice areas that exist, and how those roles work in those different areas. You can be an entertainment lawyer and work at a firm. You can be an entertainment lawyer and work in-house. You can be an entertainment lawyer and work for yourself. Also, you should have an idea of what part of the industry you may want to pursue. Do you want to be in music? Do you want to be in film and TV? Do you want to be in media? Do you want to be in advertising? Where is your passion? Where is your interest?

Finding your specific interest area requires some additional work. If you are interested in practicing Entertainment Law, Google what entertainment attorneys do. Determine if what you have identified is interesting to you. Based on your interest, you can start looking into roles that are in line with your interest and learn more about what those role entails. Start reaching out to attorneys in that space to get more information. Do your homework!

What characteristics are important for those considering law firm ownership?

Beyond knowing the law or being familiar with the practice of law, if you want to own your law firm, you also need to understand how to run a business. I think it is imperative that you understand that. I speak to a lot of lawyers that go out on their own, and they underestimate the business side of law firm ownership. You are running a business. You are marketing your business. You are the accountant for your business. You are doing everything to run a business. The other side of the learning process is making sure that you know how to run a business.

In owning a firm, you must know what your strengths are and be able to lean into them and know your weaknesses to properly get assistance where needed. You have to be a great lawyer AND a great businessperson.

What have you learned in 20 years that will be helpful for those considering law firm ownership and what advice would you give to those considering law firm ownership?

Make sure to be clear about your fees, your billing, and your retainer. Many lawyers, in whatever practice area they are

PILLAR 10 - IT TAKES A VILLAGE

in, get into law because they want to help and serve their clients. However, you must make sure that you are still being business-minded and do not compromise your time or your fees. You must value your time and properly bill for your time. Many solos tend to under-bill or under-record their time. It is important to get paid for all your time, especially when you are working for yourself. Know your numbers.

If you have a limited business background, I also suggest that you consider taking business classes, accounting classes, and marketing classes. There is a wealth of resources out there.

Also, do your research on operational costs. Really think about how you will organize your business and figure out the cost of running your business. You need to know how much money you must bring in to make a profit. Think about what that looks like; how many clients or matters you must take on to make your projected, desired profit. Consider that in deciding your hourly rate, your retainer, or however you decide to bill for your time. Get an idea of how much work you need to do to have the lifestyle that you want, to pay your bills, and to live the life you want.

Do the numbers and know that there are always going to be ups and downs. Business will not be consistent all the time. For instance, I had to learn to calculate my annual revenue based on 11 months a year, excluding December, because the entertainment business slows down at the end of the year, and so there are not a lot of checks being cut. I had to factor that into my revenue estimates. Learn your business so you are aware of the slow periods and the peak periods.

Again, if numbers and finances are not your strength, get help!

Do you believe women face more challenges setting their fees and respecting their time?

Absolutely. I think it is more difficult for women because we naturally want to be helpful. There might be an occasion where our fees exceed our initial retainer, and as women, we do not feel comfortable going back to the client and asking for the additional money for our services. Women also tend to undervalue themselves overall anyway. As an attorney and businessperson, you must push past that. Do not undervalue your time or underestimate your time.

How do you deal with being a powerhouse attorney, business owner, and an all-around boss woman? Do you find it harder to date?

I have found that it can be harder to date. For one, there is a perception in general of what lawyers are, our personality, etc. I mean, honestly, we kind of get a bad rap in general.

Based on the generalizations about lawyers, it can be hard if you are out meeting men, and you share with someone that you are a lawyer, and they categorize who you are based on what you do. Sometimes men will apply their preconceived notions of what being a lawyer means on to you personally or your interactions. For example, I hate when a guy says something like, "Oh you are a lawyer, so you must like to argue." You have to explain to them that what you do is different from who you are. In the past, I have avoided initially telling men what I do. I may say I work in the entertainment business. However, if a guy is only focused on what you do, he is probably not the guy for you anyway.

Do you believe men are intimidated by your success?

That is a hard one because I tend to not buy into the idea that men are intimidated by women. But I do think that there are perceptions that reflect that. I do think that there are men—generally, not specifically—that are insecure enough with themselves, so that dating someone that is accomplished scares them. Dating someone that makes more money than them scares them. Dating someone that is more educated than them scares them. And so, then they may be intimated.

I also think that men must understand that you are not dating a "lawyer" persona, you are dating a woman who is a lawyer. Are you intimidated by me or are you just intimidated by what I do? For example, Shawn Carter is married to Beyoncé Knowles. Beyoncé Knowles is not married to Jay-Z. Shawn is not married to Beyoncé. Their occupation is what they do—they are artists. At home, they are just Shawn and Bey.

Any last words?

It is very empowering and awesome to work for yourself if you can figure it out and really commit to it. You must know yourself enough to know that you can do it, and identify what you cannot do. Do not be deterred by others who say it is hard. It is hard, but if you take the time, learn best practices, and do the work, then you can have success. It is great to choose this as an option if you really want it. However, it's disappointing that we have so many statistics of women really defaulting into launching their own practices because they are not getting the support or feeling included in big firms, so they feel like they need to leave and start their own firms. I want women to feel empowered and make the decision to choose law firm ownership from a mindset of "I want to own my own firm, and I am ready to do it."

Nyanza Shaw's Bio:

Nyanza Shaw, Esq., Owner/Managing Partner of Shaw Esquire, is a well-respected entertainment and business attorney with a wealth of experience in the areas of Entertainment and Business Law, intellectual property, technology, media, and brand strategy. The firm provides legal representation to content creators, entrepreneurs, businesses, brands, and founders as well as business consulting and brand management services. Ms. Shaw also serves as outside General Counsel to several business clients, which includes providing them with advice on legal and business affairs, brand strategy, regulatory compliance, and IP portfolio management. Ms. Shaw frequently writes articles and speaks on topics related to Entertainment and Business Law, intellectual property, branding, and media. She currently serves as President of the John M. Langston Bar Association, is a member of the California State Bar's Law Practice Management and Technology Executive Committee (and Past Chair), and serves on the boards of Reading Partners LA and Our Girls Enrich, as well as volunteers with several other organizations. Ms. Shaw received her BA from Mills College and her JD from UC Hastings College of the Law.

IG/Twitter/Facebook @shawesquire.com

INTERVIEW 7
ESTEEMED CRIMINAL DEFENSE ATTORNEY, PAMELA DANDSBY

What are your practice areas, and why did you select those areas?

Well, my practice areas currently are Criminal Law and Family Law. I started in Criminal Law as a public defender for 10 years. When I left the office, I had no intention of practicing in any area other than Criminal Law. However, before I left the office, a friend of mine from college wanted to get divorced, and he requested my assistance.

Initially, when he requested my assistance, I declined. At the time I did not know much about Family Law. Even when I told him that, he begged me and told me he trusted me. So, finally, I said "yes." It seemed like every Family Law issue you could have in one case, I experienced. That is how I started practicing Family Law. I had to learn so much. I was up against a gentleman who was such a pit bull, and he had been practicing for maybe 30 years in Family Law. It was very intimidating, but we got through it, and successfully.

Why did you decide after ten years at the Public Defender's Office to go out on your own?

I did consider going out on my own after five years in practice, but at the time, I did not know anything about handling my own practice or running my own business. I had only been practicing for five years. I felt rather confident that I knew what I was doing in terms of the work but not as much as I did five years later when I left. I also considered the possible financial impact, considering I was a single mom.

By the time I left the office, my son's dad had stopped paying child support, and it was scary to think about the financial ramifications at the time. Literally, I was scared.

By ten years, I knew it was time. I wanted to have closer contact with my clients than I did at the Public Defender's Office, and I wanted the flexibility with my son. At that time, my son was six years old and needed more help with homework, extracurricular activities, etc. I had accumulated a good amount of savings, and I also had equity in my home. I wanted to make sure I had something to fall back on. So, by that time, I had a line of credit, just in case things did not work out or business was slow. My research revealed the common experience was, "You do not make money for the first six months to a year." So, I had that in mind.

I had also read books by that time on starting a law practice. Once I felt financially secure and I knew a basic outline of how to do it through reading the books and talking to people, I was ready to open my practice. During this time, I met an older attorney who became a mentor and close friend. I interviewed him as well, and he helped me with the transition.

How was your first year of practice?

I got a small office and kept things quite simple. At the time, I believe I had a case management system, a desk, internet, phone, and that's it. So, as a single mother, that helped a lot to keep my expenses low because, although I did not make a whole lot of money, I did earn enough to cover my expenses.

I continued my Criminal Law work and Family Law, and I was also introduced to civil litigation.

PILLAR 10 – IT TAKES A VILLAGE

When I first came out, I knew a guy who was a vice president of a small corporation. His corporation had been sued at the time. He wanted me to file an Answer to the Complaint. Again, like the Family Law case, I did not know what to do. But I researched my options and went for it.

Saying "yes" to this opportunity was one of the best decisions that I made for my firm because the company continued to hire me for their cases. I essentially became their general counsel for about five years.

In addition to civil litigation, how did you get clients the first year in the other areas of practice?

For criminal cases, the Los Angeles County Bar Association has a program, the Indigent Criminal Defense Association, commonly referred to as Bar Panel or ICDA. It is a panel of attorneys that are appointed on cases when the Public Defender or the Alternate Public Defender cannot take a case. So, for example, if three people are arrested, the Public Defender takes the first defendant, the Alternate Public Defender takes another, and I may be assigned the third person who needs an attorney.

Even though I was on the panel, the computer company I represented my first year out kept me very busy, and the Family Law kept me very busy. But as time went on, I began using the panel a lot more. The panel did not pay a lot, but for my first year, it was worth it.

I also placed my business card in a local newspaper, and I received cases from that posting. The editor of the newspaper also referred clients. When I first started, attorneys still advertised in the phone book, so I also advertised in the phone book for about two years.

I purposely located my office in Pasadena because that is where I grew up, and I know a lot of people, so I picked up several cases from family and friends as well.

As my practice grew and I assisted more clients, my client referral base grew. As such, a lot of my current business comes from referrals, and I have also joined another panel for juvenile criminal law cases.

How was that for you starting a new practice and being a single parent?

It was hard. It was really hard, but I always knew, no matter what, that I was going to be there for my son. And I was comfortable with not making as much money as I could have. For several years, I have never wanted to sacrifice my time with him. As I mentioned, throughout my career, I continued to keep my expenses down, so the income I earned continued to cover those expenses and allowed me to live comfortably while being intentionally present for my son.

What other challenges did you face running your own practice in the beginning?

It was beautiful. I did not have any challenges, initially. I loved doing the work. I loved coming in on the weekends, five to six hours on Saturday, it didn't bother me. But two years later when the recession hit, that was devastating... between 2007 and 2009. People did not have money to hire attorneys, one. And then, two, for some reason (I do

PILLAR 10 - IT TAKES A VILLAGE

not know why it coincided with the recession), but in 2008, the criminal law panel did not have many cases to distribute to the panel attorneys. Typically, as in 2007, the panel had approximately 30,000 cases to distribute among the attorneys. The next year, in 2008, the number of cases decreased by half. So you can only imagine the competition for those cases. The panel had to change the whole distribution format. So, in 2007 and 2008, I experienced financial devastation. Those two years were extremely difficult for my practice. As you know, when you are financially stressed, that stress can impact all areas of your life, so it was challenging. But I continued to do what I needed to do and rode the wave. It took a long time to recover from that, but I did it.

Did you ever consider going back to the Public Defender's Office or going to work for a firm?

Yes. In 2017 or 2018, I considered it because I had a friend who started at the Public Defender's Office with me who later went to work for the district attorney's office in San Bernardino for several years. Over the years, he would always call on me to join him, but I did not want to be a district attorney; he then offered to assist my placement at the San Bernardino Public Defender's Office.

What about single mothers considering law firm ownership, what is your advice for them?

Take the time to plan your move down to the penny. And I say that because I did plan my moves, but I did not do so down to the penny, and I wish I would have. Make sure you plan where you are going to have your office space.

Consider: How much is your office space? How much are your computers? Where are you going to get your furniture? What's the best phone and internet package? Are there other attorneys in the building with whom I can brainstorm? All of these things. And try to think of every single extra expense you may unexpectedly encounter.

So, in short, I would just make sure you think everything through.

Watch your expenses. If possible, attempt to have money saved or a line of credit so you do have a cushion if you face any financial challenges, which most of us do in the early years.

As a single mother, if you don't have a really close family member that can help you with your child, like your mother or your sister, I would urge you to go slow and keep your children your priority. You can try to make as much money as you can, but do not make that your priority, so that you can spend time with your children. If you do have a trustworthy support system, although your children will miss you, if they have solid and loving care, you will feel a little better about doing what you need to do for your practice.

I would also encourage single moms to enroll their children in some type of activity/sports, and that way, your children enjoy the sports/activity and that gives you that much more time to get work done. Even if you go to their practices, you can take your work with you. Small things add up, like reading cases or emailing clients/opposing counsel, etc. Also, use the after-care programs at school some days, which will also allow you to get more done. Those of us with children must work smarter, not harder. But the transition gets better as children get older and become more independent.

A lot of attorneys do not proceed because of fear, what are your thoughts on fear?

I think the fear can be combatted by planning. Interview and shadow other solo attorneys in your practice area. Learn every aspect of running a law practice before you make your final move. I had so very many people that I could call and ask questions. I had a friend who I would always ask about civil matters. Another friend, I would call about family law questions. I even approached attorneys I did not know. They all will be happy to share their knowledge. Particularly for those opening a practice straight out of law school, it will be priceless to go into court and watch how judges handle the cases.

The fear begins to dissipate because you know what to do. But there is only so much comfort you can get before you jump out.

If you have your money in place, you have your systems in place, and you have your network in place, you will be better prepared than most.

How do you balance family, law firm ownership, and maintaining your marriage?

Well, I have only been married now for four months. I have absolutely no issue with it because he was in the same exact position. He was a criminal defense attorney, and he did some civil litigation as well as a solo practitioner and had a partner for several years prior to being a solo practitioner.

Not only does he get it, but he is so proud of me, encourages me, and supports me. It is beautiful in that regard.

In marriage, there are many people who are old school traditional, and then there's new school, and then there is something in the middle, hybrids. If you are rather traditional like my mom, she was a stay-at-home mom, and she never worked outside of the home, except for one year when I was in high school. She was a real estate agent. I tend to be more traditional, but at the same time, obviously, I did not like the tradition 100% because not only do I work, I have my own business.

At the end of the day, there must be a discussion about the shift of responsibilities, etc., and the rearranging of expectations. The failure to communicate about changing roles can really be a problem.

For those with less supportive spouses or those not in the legal field, how does one talk to their spouse about law firm ownership?

I think it is important to discuss how your spouse feels about your decision. If the parties can get on the same page about how things will be moving forward, how things may change, the discussion of finances, the discussion of the shift in roles, the parties may be more prepared.

If you face challenges, it may be a good idea to speak to a therapist or trusted advisor, even if you have a great marriage or you don't generally need therapy. Therapy on that issue alone (i.e., planning the transition and managing expectations), can assist in the transition.

PILLAR 10 - IT TAKES A VILLAGE

And, discuss everything! Discuss all possibilities, starting with finances, because the business may not take off initially. Also discuss how the responsibilities for the children will change. Discuss work hours. What are the hours you are working and not working, not just in the office, but taking calls on your cell phone and working from home? A Sunday morning call during family time can lead to a point of frustration in a relationship.

Work can also affect your vacation and family time. I remember a time I was literally backing out of my driveway, going on vacation for a week when a friend called me, absolutely frantic about his new job doing a background check. I had to spend some of my vacation working on his case. Again, have a discussion with your spouse about handling these emergency cases that will arise in your practice.

Pam Dansby's Bio:

Ms. Dansby graduated from UCLA with an Economics degree 1990, followed by a juris doctorate degree from Loyola Law School in 1994. She became a Los Angeles County Deputy Public Defender in 1995, where she handled all stages of misdemeanors and serious/violent felonies. In 2000, she continued to master complex felony litigation at the Alternate Public Defender's Office. In 2005, she launched her solo firm.

As a solo practitioner, Ms. Dansby continued her criminal practice, handling high level private and court-appointed felonies, with the majority of her criminal defense clients facing life imprisonment. She expanded her practice beyond Criminal Defense to include Family Law and civil litigation. Ms. Dansby has litigated hundreds of trials and contested hearings in all areas of practice.

In her personal time, she has served as Chairperson of the Board of Outward Bound Adventures, President of the Board of Pasadena Rosebud Academy, and co-chaired or served on committees on the Board of Black Woman Lawyers, Inc. and California Women Lawyers. Ms. Dansby has been recognized by The Pasadena Journal, "Accomplished African Americans Under 40," The Pasadena Weekly, "Best Attorney 2016," and Black Faces Magazine, "2020 Influential 50." Ms. Dansby is regularly invited to speak on legal matters.

PILLAR 10

1. *What have I learned from the attorney interviews that I can incorporate in my own law firm?*

The Completed Outline!
Here it is ....

MY LAW FIRM BLUEPRINT

PILLAR 1

1. What is my "Why"?
2. What are my fears?
3. What are my limiting beliefs?

PILLAR 2

WRITE OUT my commitment contract to myself and my practice.

PILLAR 3

Interview with Three Attorneys

1.
2.
3.

Legal name

1. What names are fitting for my law practice?

    1)

    2)

    3)

    4)

    5)

2. Are the names selected available?
3. What steps do I need to take to legally own my selected name?
4. What names do my trusted mentors/friends like best?

Business formation

Business professional I will meet:

1. Based on my meeting with the business professional, what corporation is best for my business?
2. Will I incorporate the business myself, or will I hire someone to do this step for me?

Business taxes

CPA professionals I will meet:

1.

2.

3.

After my meeting:

1. What are my tax obligations based on my corporation?

THE COMPLETE OUTLINE

2. Do I need a business license?
3. Am I required to pay city taxes?
4. What is my tax obligation if I hire employees?
5. How often should I meet with my CPA?

City licensing fees

1. Does my city require a business license?
2. If so, what fees am I responsible for each year?

Managing business income/expenses

1. How will I track my business income?
2. How will I track my business expenses?
3. Will I hire a part-time bookkeeper or do this myself?

Bank accounts and credit cards

1. Where will I maintain my business bank account?
2. Do I need to maintain an IOTA account? Does my bank know how to properly set up the IOTA account?
3. Do I need a business credit card?

Payroll

1. How often will I pay myself and my staff?
2. Will I handle payroll, or will I hire someone to assist me?
3. How will I take care of my payroll taxes?

Insurance

1. Will I maintain legal malpractice insurance?

2. If so, five companies in my area that offer affordable legal malpractice insurance are:

   1)

   2)

   3)

   4)

   5)

3. Do I need Workers' Compensation insurance for my employees?

4. If so, five companies in my area that offer affordable Workers' Compensation insurance are:

   1)

   2)

   3)

   4)

   5)

PILLAR 4

The budget

1. What are my fixed personal expenses?
2. What are my adjustable personal expenses?
3. What are my business expenses?
4. What is my projected business income?
5. In the event I am unable to cover my expenses, then what?

THE COMPLETE OUTLINE

What is my billing structure?

1. The hourly rate?
2. If so, what is my hourly rate?
3. A flat fee?
4. If so, what is my flat fee rate for each service that I provide?
5. How many hours should I bill each month?

Retainer and retainer agreement

1. Will I charge a retainer?
2. How much is my retainer?
3. Will I require full payment for the retainer, or will I accept payments?
4. Does my firm require a retainer agreement?
5. What are the terms of my retainer agreement?

Practice area

1. What is my practice area?
2. Do I want to change my practice area?
3. What other areas do I want to consider?
   1)
   2)
   3)

Partnerships

1. Will I have a partner?
2. Why or why not?

3. How will I select my partner?
4. Potential partners:
   1)
   2)
   3)

Office space/location

1. Do I need additional office space?
2. Can my office operate remotely?
3. What is the best office location for my firm?

Employees

1. Do I need to hire employees right now?
2. If so, whom do I need to hire?
   1)
   2)
   3)
3. How much will I pay each employee?

Systems

1. What systems do I need for my practice?
   1)
   2)
   3)
   4)
   5)

THE COMPLETE OUTLINE

6)

7)

Professional development

1. How will I continue to professionally advance my career?

   1)

   2)

   3)

   4)

   5)

   6)

   7)

PILLAR 5

1. What is my brand marketing plan?

2. How will I market the practice?

   1)

   2)

   3)

   4)

   5)

PILLAR 6

1. Do I have a book of business, or do I need to start from the beginning?

2. How many clients will I have the day I open my doors?
3. How will I manage potential clients and clients?
4. What is my system for all potential clients?
5. What is my system for scheduling potential clients?
6. What is my system for the client that wants to retain my firm?
7. What is my system for the client that wants to think about hiring my firm?
8. What is the close out process for the client who did not hire my firm?

PILLAR 7

1. What do I need to prepare for my first court experience?
2. Am I familiar with my judicial officer?
3. How will I respond to any negativity that may arise?
4. Have I prepared my client for what to expect at the hearing?

PILLAR 8

1. What are my priorities?
2. What is myself-care routine?
3. How will I continue to enjoy my life?

PILLAR 9

1. How will I implement the above lessons for my firm's success?

THE COMPLETE OUTLINE

PILLAR 10

1. *What have I learned from the attorney interviews that I can incorporate in my own law firm?*

You did it! You made it through all 10 pillars and have a working outline and tools to get your started on your law firm journey! I hope you have gained the confidence you need to take the leap of faith and feel confident to move forward with the information provided.

I would LOVE to hear about your success. I can be found at Demetria.gravesesq@gmail.com for now. LOL. I wish you the best of luck, and I can't wait to hear from you!

Made in United States
Troutdale, OR
06/24/2023

The Gods' Own County

A Heathen Prayer Book

Dan Coultas
&
Heathens of Yorkshire

First edition
Published 2019 by Heathens of Yorkshire

◉Follow us on Instagram @thegodsowncounty

fFollow our Facebook page fb.me/thegodsowncounty

Cover art by Art by Eleanor Rose

◉Follow them on Instagram @_artbyeleanorose

Internal illustrations by The Saxon Storyteller

◉Follow them on Instagram @thesaxonstoryteller

Copyright © 2019 Heathens of Yorkshire

All rights reserved. No part of this book, including all artwork, may be reprinted or reproduced or utilised in any form or by any electronic, mechanical, or other means, now known or hereafter invented, including photocopying and recording, or in any information storage or retrieval system, without permission in writing from Heathens of Yorkshire.

To the fullest extent of the law, neither the authors, contributors or editors assume any liability for any injury and/or damage to persons or property as a matter of products liability, negligence or otherwise, or from any use or operation of any methods, products, instructions, or ideas contained in the material herein.

ISBN: 9781090821980

Wights of Yorkshire,
Ancestors whose feet walked our ancient land, hail!
See here the banner of our kith.
The white rose of Yorkshire,
Symbolising our history, our culture, our people.
The wolves, Freki and Geri,
Symbolising our dedication to the Gods.
The name,
Which ties us together in frith, kith and kin.
Bless this banner,
Let it represent our strength, our customs and our values,
Let all who gaze upon it know who we are;
For we are the Heathens of Yorkshire!

Contents

Banner Blessing..iii

Contents...iv

Introduction..1

Creation of Sacred Space..4

Ægir..5
Lord of Hosts..6
Father of the Waves..7

Baldur..8
Fairest of Face, Fairest of Voice..9
Lord of Breidablik – *Keith Leggott*..10

Bragi..11
Greatest of Skalds...12
The Skald's Call...13

Brigantia...14
Ancient Lady of the North..15

Eir...16
White Rose Healer..17
Healer of the Broken...18
An Ode to Eir – *Alda Björk Ólafsdóttir*..19

Ēostre..21
Bringer of the Dawn...22
Blót to Ostara – *Neil Coultas*...23

Forseti...24
Greatest of Mediators...25
Safeguarding Ties of Kinship..26

Freyja..27
First Chooser of the Slain...28
Lady of Fölkvangr...29
Goddess of Passion...30

Freyr 31
Bestower of Peace and Pleasure 32
Lord of Alfheim 33
Lord of Peace – *Al Daw* 34
Lord of the Yule Feast 35
A Time to Sow 36
A Time to Reap 37
Ode to Ingui – *James Batty* 38

Frigg 39
Lady of the Hearth 40
Mother of Mothers 41
The Handmaidens of Frigg 42

Heimdallr 43
The Rainbow 44
Watchman of the Gods 45
The White God – *Keith Leggott* 46

Hel 47
A Traveller Approaches 48
Goddess of the Underworld – *Keith Leggott* 49
Host to the Dead – *Keith Leggott* 50

The Hosts of the Dead 51
A Warm Place by the Fire 52
A Warrior Has Left Us 53

Idunna 54
Sustainer of the Gods 55
Keeper of the Fruit – *Keith Leggott* 56

Jörð 57
Earth Mother 58
Hostess of the Living 59
Jörð our Home – *Kristian Lewin-Petrov* 60

Kvasir 61
Wisest of the Gods 62

Loki 63
Catalyst of Greatness 64
Lord of Self-Sacrifice – *Keith Leggott* 65
Trickster & Adventurer – *Keith Leggott* 66
Shaver of the Golden Hair – *Keith Leggott* 67
Misunderstood by the Majority – *Keith Leggott* 68

Mani **69**
Celestial Guide 70
A Familiar Face 71

Njörð **72**
Lord of Nótún 73
Sharer of Wealth 74
Protector of the Boundary 75

The Norns **76**
A Turn of Your Spindle 77
At the Roots of the World Tree 78

Odin **79**
Wise One of Many Names 80
Lord of War 81
Lord of the Long Night 82
Facing the Enemy Within 83
Son of Bor – *Keith Leggott* 84
Lord of Valhalla – *Keith Leggott* 85

Rán **86**
Queen of the Deep 87
We Journey to Your Realm 88
Giving Thanks for Safe Passage 89
A Kinsman at Your Door 90

Seaxnēat **91**
You Guide our Tribe – *Tara Skinner* 92
Your People Will Not Forget You 93

Sif **94**
Rowan Lady 95
Goddess of the Harvest Hair – *Keith Leggott* 96

Skaði **97**
Þjazi's Brave Daughter 98
Bringer of Warmth to Our Hearts 99
Giantess From the Cold – *Keith Leggott* 100
Wife of Njörð – *Keith Leggott* 101

Sunna **102**
Lady of Light, Lady of Life 103
A Glimpse of Your Face 104

Thor **105**
Friend to the Sons & Daughters of the Earth 106
Protector of Gods & Men 107
A Prayer to Thor – *Daniel Warden* 108
Protector of Man & Asgard – *Keith Leggott* 109
Wielder of Mjölnir – *Keith Leggott* 110
The Companions of Thor 111
Fair Winds & Following Seas 112
Lord of Bilskirnir – *Keith Leggott* 113

Tyr **114**
Friend of the Wolf 115
Most Honourable of the Æsir 116
The Disabled Warrior – *Keith Leggott* 117

Ullr **118**
Dweller of the Yew Dale 119

Var **120**
An Oath Sworn 121

Vidar **122**
God of Vengeance 123
After the Destruction and the Flame 124

The Wights **125**
The Waterwights 126
An Unfamiliar Place 127
Guests in Your Home 128
The Housewights 129
Wights of the Tavern 130
Wights of the North 131

The Ancestors **132**
The Disir 133
The Alfar 134
The Einherjar 135
Our Ever-Present Guides 136

Military Prayers **137**
Naval Prayer 138
A Soldier's Prayer 139
Royal Marine Prayer 140
Submariner's Prayer 141
Air Force Prayer 142

Songs & Poems **143**
Thank the Gods It's Yule 144
Heathens o' Yorkshire 146
Viking Soul - *Alda Björk Ólafsdóttir* 148
The Tears of the Wolf - *Alda Björk Ólafsdóttir* 149
Cries of the Heart - *Alda Björk Ólafsdóttir* 151
Gifts of the Goddesses – *Adrian Spendlow* 153

Rituals **155**
A Blót to Thor 156
Midsummer Blót to Sunna 160
Harvest Blót 162
Heathen Remembrance Service 164
Mothers' Night Blót 169
Yule Blót to Odin 171
Naming Ceremony 174
Home Blessing Ritual 177
Wedding Ceremony 179
Funeral 182

About Heathens of Yorkshire **186**

INTRODUCTION

This book has been a labour of love, put together over many months. When Heathens of Yorkshire first formed, and started holding our own blóts, we used prayers and invocations written by others. The first one I wrote myself was only done out of necessity, as there was no heathen prayer available to the deity we wanted to invoke. This was hardly surprising, as it was Brigantia, the ancient Goddess of the Celtic tribe the Brigantes, who once inhabited a large area of northern England, including Yorkshire.

This prayer was incorporated into a blót at one of our camps, and was very well received. From there I started writing prayers to Gods and Goddesses I felt particularly strong connections with, and incorporating these into our rituals. As time went on, a collection was built up, until we eventually reached the point where we could use all our own words in our rituals. At some point, probably by a fire, and after a fair few honey based beverages, someone suggested we compiled all the words we had into a book. Not only for our own members, but also for heathens everywhere, so that they too could benefit from prayers and invocations we had created, and draw inspiration for writing their own.

Having put the word out for contributors, we received some excellent pieces from our members. We also decided that we wanted to make this book truly special; we wanted it to be something that heathens everywhere will want to have in their collection, and so not only did we decide to add songs and complete rituals to the book, we decided that the book should be fully illustrated. I would like to personally thank all our authors, Keith Leggott, Alda Björk Ólafsdóttir, Adrian Spendlow, Kristian Lewin-Petrov, Daniel Warden, Al Daw, James Batty, Neil Coultas and Tara Skinner, as well as our artists, Matt Greenway (The Saxon Storyteller) and Thea Wilby (Art by Eleanor Rose), who have truly brought this book alive.

All writing in this book is my own work unless it states that it is by another one of our members mentioned above. For the words I have written I have drawn on my own experience of working with the Gods, Goddesses, wights and ancestors, as well as existing literary sources for inspiration. In places I have created my own kennings, in others I have drawn on existing kennings from the eddas and sagas. In some places I have borrowed phrases from various rune poems. For the military prayers and remembrance service I have taken existing pieces and adapted them to make them applicable to heathens. I will leave it to those of you who are familiar with Yorkshire culture to guess which tune I have used for the Heathens of Yorkshire song!

When it comes to the names of the deities, I have not stuck rigidly to a particular convention. For deities who feature exclusively in Saxon sources, I have used the Saxon name. For most of the Gods and Goddesses I have used the name that I know them by, which in most, but not all cases is the anglicised version of the Old Norse name. Some people may not be happy with this, but to me the meaning behind the words is far more important than what spelling of a name is used. We cannot possibly know what version of their names, if any, the Gods use themselves, and so I don't think it is worth making this a sticking point.

As well as the authors and artists, there are several other people without whom this book would not have been possible. I would like to thank all of the members of Heathens of Yorkshire for convincing me to keep writing, and to put this book together for the community. I would like to thank the group's kindred council for all their support throughout the project, and in particular those members of the kindred who are also my family, Sabrina Coultas and Robin Smith, for all their help in proof reading and keeping me plied with endless cups of Yorkshire tea!

I would also like to acknowledge the authors whose work I used back in the days before I was writing my own prayers for the blóts I was putting together for the group. Patricia M Lafayllve whose 'Practical Heathen's Guide to Asatru' contains a great beginner's guide to writing rituals, and Hester Butler-Ehle, whose own heathen prayer book, 'Hearth and Field', was not only very useful when writing blóts in the past, but was also the inspiration behind putting this book together in the first place. As well as these authors, I would like to thank Geoff Miles, Phil Parkyn and Jack Hudson from Asatru UK, with whom I have exchanged ritual notes in the past, and whose rituals I have attended on many occasions. Finally I'd like to thank AUK chair Rich Blackett for all his advise on the technical aspects of putting this book together.

This book has several key aims. Firstly to provide the heathen community as a whole with what we sincerely hope will be a useful resource in putting together their own rituals. Secondly to raise money for Heathens of Yorkshire, with all profits made going to support the group's ongoing projects. Finally, and most importantly, the purpose of this book is to honour our Gods and Goddesses, the wights and the ancestors.

Hail the Æsir! Hail the Vanir! Hail the wights and the ancestors! Hail Yorkshire!

-Dan Coultas, Goði of Heathens of Yorkshire

Creation of Sacred Space

These words can be used at the beginning of a ritual as a means of creating sacred space, and focusing the energy of the participants.

There were once but two realms, separated by a great, inconceivable void. The endless, baron chasm called Ginnungagap. To one side lay the icy, frozen land of Niflheim, too cold for any creature to survive. On the other, Muspelheim lay, where the raging fires prevented even the hardiest of life. When these forces finally met, so the first being was created, the first of the mighty giants, Ymir.

Nurtured by the great cow, Audhumla, Ymir spawned the race of giants. Audhumla licked at the ice for her own sustenance, and slowly but surely released Buri, first of the Æsir, from his frozen prison. Buri bore a son, Bor, who, with the giantess Bestla, bore three sons, Odin, Vili and Ve.

The three brothers grew, and once they were strong enough, rose up and slew the great Ymir, and with his corpse created a home. That home, is our home, where we are born, where we will die, where we will see great joy, where we will suffer terrible hardship, and where we will witness every emotion. From Ymir's skull, they created the sky above us, from his brains came the clouds, which give us the rains. His muscles formed the land on which we live, and the blood that poured from his wounds that day was to become the great oceans.

Having made our home, they made us. From a trunk of ash, and a trunk of elm, they made Ask and Embla, the first of our human ancestors. Their descendants would later mate with Rígr, to make us who we are today, not just creations of the Gods, but distant relatives. Here we stand, as our ancestors stood, the product of the Gods, in the home the Gods fought to create for us. Here we stand, as our descendants will stand, to honour the Gods, wights and ancestors, until the chaos returns, and the realms of Gods and men fall.

Ægir

Lord of Hosts

Hail to noble Ægir!
Host of lords, lord of hosts.
Friend to Æsir and Vanir alike;
All the Gods gladly gather in your hall,
To sample your legendary hospitality,
And your legendary mead!
Master brewer,
No earthly brew comes close to yours,
No earthly gathering can be as mirthful,
As those you host below the smooth path of ships.
We thank you for showing us how to treat or guests,
We thank you for sharing the secret of the honey wave.
Hail Ægir!

Father of the Waves

Hail to Ægir, Lord of the deep.
Egil's foe,
Your power has no earthly match.
Father of the waves,
Your daughters are both beautiful and fearsome.
Brother of fire and of wind,
Yours are the mysteries of the prow road.
When the Gods of Asgard look to gather,
There is no finer venue than gold lit Brime,
No sweeter refreshment than the nectar of Hyme's kettle,
No greater beauty than Rán your bride.
Whilst all the lands of the earth have felt the footsteps of mankind,
You guard the secrets below.
Hail Ægir!

Baldur

Fairest of Face, Fairest of Voice

Hail to Baldur the bright!
Hail to Baldur the beautiful!
Hail to Baldur the brave!
Fairest of face, fairest of voice,
None amongst the Gods speak ill of you.
So beloved of fair Frigg,
She sought to protect you from all the worlds ills,
But the mistletoe would be your bane.
We know not what your father whispered in your ear,
As you began your journey to Hel.
The Gods tried in vain to bring you back from that place,
But you will rise again.
Out of the ashes of Sutr's fire,
Out of the rubble of Asgard,
Out of the battlefield strewn with the corpses of the Gods,
You will rise again,
To take your fathers throne,
So that there will be life once more.
Hail Baldur!

Lord of Breidablik
-Keith Leggott

Hail to Baldur!
The Golden-Haired God, favourite of Frigg.
Husband to Nanna, father to Forseti, the oath keeper,
Twin to Hodur, whose home is the palace of Breidablik,
With its silver roof and golden pillars.
Owner of Ringhorn, the greatest of all ships.
Son of Odin, son of Frigg.
Beloved by Gods and man.
To Baldur,
So beloved that every creature promised Frigg to do you no harm.
Your dreams of the prophecy of your death made you invincible,
Thus teaching us that no situation is entirely hopeless;
There is always room for optimism.
It also instructed us never to be over-confident,
As the opposite is also true.
If indestructible has the slightest weakness, it shall be discovered.
Hail to Baldur: given a send-off truly fit for a God.
We learn from you fortitude as you wait patiently with Nanna,
To be returned to the world after Ragnarok.
We thank you Baldur for the lessons you teach us,
And we leave you this offering as a thank you.

Bragi

Greatest of Skalds

Hail Bragi, greatest of skalds!
First maker of poetry,
You are the master of the spoken word.
Tales of heroes and Gods alike come alive,
Re-lived by the hearth fire on a long winter's night.
Reputations secured to the sound of your lire,
Entertainment brought to the mead hall.
Long bearded God,
You are renowned for your wisdom,
As well as your skill with words.
All those who seek to share stories,
Would do well to seek your patronage.
Husband of fair Idunn,
You possess eloquence surpassing all others.
Hail Bragi!

The Skald's Call

Hail Bragi!
The warriors are gathered in the hearth ship,
The yeast's flood flows,
As the hounds hunt for scraps in the floor rushes.
The ring giver stands, and calls for silence,
For now is the time for the blood of Kvasir.
Bragi, Odinson, king of skalds,
At this moment the skilled smith of poetry silently calls to you,
Asks that you guide their tongue,
Sharpen their wit,
And fill them with the confidence to entertain.
As poets, as singers, as writers, we call to you Bragi,
We ask that you share but a fraction of your skill with us,
That we do not spout the dung of the ancient eagle!
Wordsmith, linguist, eloquent brother of the thunderer,
Whose weapon is the sword of the gums,
We thank you for the gift of the spoken word.
Hail Bragi!

Brigantia

Ancient Lady of the North

Hail to Brigantia,
Ancient lady of the north we call to you,
Queen of these lands,
Whose reign began long before
Our ancestors crossed the cold North Sea.
People may change, boarders may change,
But the north remains yours.
We see you in our green spaces,
On both sides of the island's spine,
We hear you in birdsong,
In the flowing of the Aire and the Mersey.
Hail to the ancient one, unchanging one, lady of the north,
Hail Brigantia!

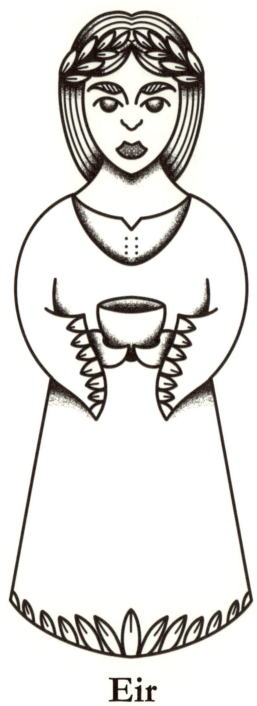

Eir

White Rose Healer

Hail to Eir, greatest of healers!
Fiery haired leech,
With the white rose,
You bring comfort to the sick,
Rest to the tired,
Peace to the dying.
Copper lady,
From Lyfjaberg you guide the doctor,
The nurse and the surgeon.
No affliction is too great,
No ailment too insignificant,
Be it of the body, or of the mind,
For your tender love and care.
Hail Eir!

Healer of the Broken

Hail Eir!
Healer of broken bodies,
Healer of broken minds.
Merciful lady,
You protect us in our time of need.
When we are weak,
When we cannot fend for ourselves,
Through an ailment,
Through an injury,
You are there.
And we thank you.
Hail Eir!

An Ode to Eir
- Alda Björk Ólafsdóttir

In this circle of trust,
We hold hands,
We strip down to our naked souls,
And humbly praise you.

You honour us with your grace,
You smile upon us with your mercy,
You love us with your protection,
Bring us peacefulness and calm.

A Valkyrie or a Goddess?
Your power is the same,
Shelter us and save us,
Eir we say your name.

Heal our souls, heal our minds,
Keep our bodies strong.
Keep us well in your embrace,
Lead us out when we do wrong.

From the hilltop of Lyfjaberg:
The hill of healing you lay,
As you and Menglöð sit side by side,
And listen to us pray.

You sit on the power of life,
And pass the sentence of death.
From kings, Gods and Goddesses,
To us the mortal souls you love no less.

The sick, sad and the wounded,
With your Eirflower you heal.
Please accept our humble offerings,
And protect us until from this earth we leave.

Offerings: Beef, goat, copper

As you shape the lives of our children.

Light some red and green candles

Our Goddess of healing,
Help us in our choices.
Help us in our struggles.
As you choose, who will live and who will die.
We are grateful for what we got,
As we put our trust in you;
As we put our trust in each other.
We raise our horn,
To our Goddess of healing:
Eir!
Góð heilsa to us all,
Góð heilsa!

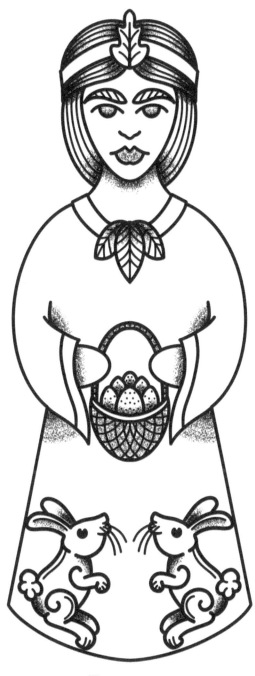

Ēostre

Bringer of the Dawn

Hail Ēostre!
Bringer of the dawn, bringer of life,
Friend of the hare, and all that is new.
As we bid farewell to Old Man Winter,
We welcome you back to the world once more.
From the east you come, bringing life,
To replenish that taken by the harsh winter cold.
Whilst many have forgotten your roots,
Your traditions have lived on,
Even amongst those who seek to destroy the old ways.
And we here know you, and we here honour you,
Oh shining lady of the dawn.
Hail Ēostre!

Blót to Ostara

-Neil Coultas

Ostara, bountiful lady, giver of life,
Goddess of the spring we call to you!

This is your time in the wheel of the year.
We feel your presence, light and darkness are once more in balance.
Old Man Winter's time is spent, for now.
Life has survived the cold and barren winter.
We welcome the coming season of warmth,
Light and beauty with the promise of good crops and plenty.
Shinning lady share your light and warmth with us this day.

This is a time of new beginning, of new life,
You bring fertility to the flowers, trees and plants,
To the birds and the beasts, who are all our brothers,
And to men and women.
To all living things.

Hail Lady Ostara.
Accept this offering of flowers and mead,
The product of your bounty.

Place flowers on altar, raise horn of mead and pour into offering bowl

All hail Lady Ostara! Hail Ostara!

Forseti

Greatest of Mediators

Hail Forseti!
Greatest of mediators, settler of disputes,
With the power to make all parties feel they have won the day.
Presiding one, bringer of justice,
Your decisions are undisputed amongst Gods and men.
Though you are kin of the Alfather,
You will not use tricks or deceit.
Instead you take time to ponder all matters,
As yours is the path of righteousness.
Son of shining Baldur and gentle Nanna,
We honour you,
And should we be judged,
we ask that we be judged fairly.
Hail Forseti!

Safeguarding Ties of Kinship

Hail Forseti!
Chairman of the assembly.
You are the great mediator,
Who settles the disputes of Gods and men.
Just one,
All who come to you in matters of law leave reconciled.
Son of shining Buldur and fair Nanna,
Dwelling in your grandfather's hall,
No argument is too heated,
No dispute too intense,
For you to defuse.
We turn to you to mend our ties of friendship,
To heal the bonds of kith and kin,
When they have been fractured,
By a matter which seems all encompassing,
But which with your help we can overcome,
So that we do not throw away that which is truly important.
Hail Forseti!

Freyja

First Chooser of the Slain

Freyja, warrior Goddess and first chooser of the slain,
For whom you weep golden tears of compassion.
We give you thanks for welcoming our glorious dead to Fölkvangr.
Queen of Valkyries, Goddess of love,
Lady of magic, we honour you.
Hail Freyja!

Lady of Földvangr

To the Lady of Földvangr hail!
Shining Freyja, first chooser of the slain,
You beauty is known throughout the nine worlds.
Njörð's daughter, with Brísingamen at your neck,
Many a God and Jotunn crave your intimate company.
Goddess of love, of seidr, of war,
Odin himself came to you,
To learn the secrets of your magic.
Mistress of cats,
You are both beautiful and fearsome.
Sensual one, fertile one, lustful one,
Not afraid of taboo.
Not afraid of the ravages of the battlefield.
Hail Freyja!

Goddess of Passion

Hail Freyja, lady of love!
Vanic goddess of passion,
You teach us to love without fear, without regret.
Beautiful lady of the Brísingamen,
Sharing your passion on your own terms,
You will not be used as a pawn in the games of the Gods.
We thank you for showing us that our love can be freely given,
And that the judgements of others matter little,
In matters of the heart.
Eagle clad Goddess of both the cat and the boar,
We thank you for showing us the strength of passion.
Hail Freyja!

Freyr

Bestower of Peace and Pleasure

Hail Freyr!
Lord of Alfheim, lord of frith,
Bountiful one, plentiful one, lustful one.
Gullinbursti's rider,
You bring life to our fields, and food to our tables.
Skiðblaðnir's master,
You bestow peace and pleasure on us all.
When you saw fair Gerd,
Your love knew no bounds.
You gave your sword,
Consigning yourself to Surtr's fire.
Prosperous one, virile one, peaceful one,
We honour you this day.
Hail Freyr!

Lord of Alfheim

We call to the lord of peace and prosperity,
To the lord of plenty, the lord passion, and of pleasure,
We call to Ingvi-Freyr!
Alfheim was your tooth gift oh fertile one,
And the alfs are your loyal subjects.
Their magic is your magic,
The magic of the land.
The magic that produces the mighty oak from the humble acorn,
That allows the cycle of the year to sustain us,
Through the constant repetition of life and death.
You know the true value of love;
You know that love is worth fighting for,
Even when you battle in vain.
Governor of the prosperity of men,
You rule over the rain and the shining of the sun,
And therewithal the fruit of the earth.
We call on you for fruitful seasons, and for peace.
We call on you when our hearts are empty,
Craving the love of another,
And we call on you to show us what we must sacrifice,
To gain our hearts' desires.
We thank you for the fruits of the earth,
We thank you for the wealth you have bestowed upon our kin,
And we thank you for the love in our hearts.
Hail Freyr!

Lord of Peace

-Al Daw

Hear us lord of prosperity!
Hear us lord of fertility!
Hear us lord of peace!
We call you to this special place to receive these gifts;
In turn bless those who are worthy with your gifts.
Let the sun shine down on fields of ripening grain,
Let tables groan with the weight of bountiful harvests,
And fertile lands.
Let household and field sing with new life,
And the joy that brings.
Hear us and know our respect.
Hail Freyr!

Lord of the Yule Feast

To the lord of the Yule feast hail!
As we gather here with our family and our kin,
We give thanks for the many blessed gifts you bestow upon us.
The boar is sacred to you,
And we are honoured to share in its bounty.
You give us the grain with which we make our bread, and our beer.
You give us peace, that we may enjoy this night in safety.
All these things you share with us, and we in turn share with you.
The nights may be long and cold,
But we gather with the ones we love,
As you have showed us how important the company of loved ones is.
Some may be far away,
But you have shown us that distance is no barrier.
We give gifts,
As you gave you sword in your quest for Gerd's fair hand.
And we give thanks, for all that we have.
Hail Freyr!

A Time to Sow

Ingvi-Freyr, we call to you!
The long winter draws to a close,
The time has come to sow the ploughed field.
To plant the crops, so that we may be sustained,
With grain, with bread, with beer.
Fertile one, we ask that you bless our fields,
We ask that your gentle rains will nurture our crops,
So that come the harvest we may feast together,
In thanks for the gifts you have bestowed upon us,
And that our stores will be full,
For another winter ahead.
Hail Freyr!

A Time to Reap

Hail to the lord of the harvest!
As the frosts melted, we asked you to fertilise our crops,
To guard the seeds as they germinated and sprouted,
To nourish the shoots with gentle rains,
And protect them as they grew.
All this you have done,
And for that we that we give thanks this day.
The time has come to harvest this crop,
The product of our shared efforts,
So that we may be sustained through the long winter.
This crop is your gift to us, and so we share it with you,
And we honour you, oh Freyr,
As we take in this crop with glad hearts.
Hail Freyr!

Ode to Ingui
-James Batty

Rode he by me in his waggon of gold,
His hair whipped by the prevailing wind.
A greater sight has never been foretold;
That great might 'neath his alabaster skin.

We followed him then o'er the great sea,
And steadily did our fortunes then grow.
Oft did we sacrifice to our Lord Ingui,
And then field after field we did sow.

As children were born unto this land,
Our cups did we raise in his name.
He held our tribe close in his hands,
And lords of all England we became.

Lost to the flow of wyrd are his many deeds,
That to our great shame are forgotten.
Yet mighty things may grow from a tiny seed,
To be sown in our fair children begotten.

Those of us who recall shall exalt him still,
And give thanks for seasons of fair weather.
His waggon tracks still lead o'er England's hills,
And his name shall be honoured forever.

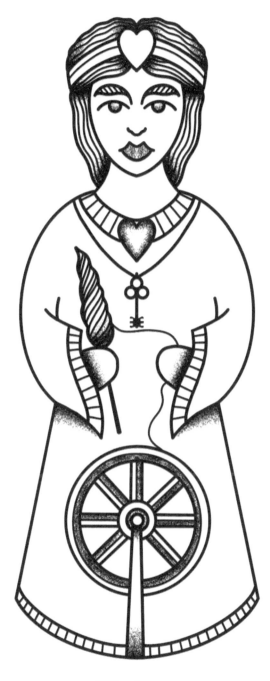

Frigg

Lady of the Hearth

Hail to Frigg!
Lady of the hearth, champion of the family, protector of women.
Keeper of the keys,
You protect our homes and strengthen our bonds of kinship,
Comforting those whose loved ones tread distant shores.
You give guidance to mothers,
Protecting and nurturing the young.
Faithful wife of Odin,
You are more than a match for his cunning.
Shining Lady of Asgard,
We honour you this night.
Hail Frigg!

Mother of Mothers

Hail to the mother of mothers!
Hail to the Queen of Asgard!
Hail to Frigg!
We call to you this mothers' night.
Caring one, kind one, loving one,
We thank you for guiding all mothers,
Giving them the strength to raise their children,
And support their families in the best way they can.
All of our mother line, going back to the beginning,
Watch over us, for we are their children.
Through your shining example they nurture us,
And help us to raise our own children,
So that our families may live forever.
Hail Frigg, mother of us all!

The Handmaidens of Frigg

Hail to the handmaidens of Frigg!
Who hold their wise Queen to be the highest authority in Asgard.
Abundant Fulla, guardian of Frigg's greatest possessions,
Gna, who carries her mistress's words across the nine worlds,
Lofn, Goddess of forbidden loves,
Syn, keeper of the boundary and protector of the hall,
Var, the oathkeeper,
Snotra, keeper of frith,
Gefjon, protector of unmarried women,
Saga, keeper of our stories and our history,
Affectionate Sjofn, goddess of the love between families and friends,
Hlin, who grants protection to those in need,
Vor, the seeress, mistress of divination,
And Eir, the white rose healer, who cares for the sick and the dying.
Goddesses of the Æsir,
Who serve Frigg dutifully,
And do so much for us.
Often overlooked, you work tirelessly regardless.
Yet we honour you this day, and we thank you.
Hail the handmaidens of Frigg!

Heimdallr

The Rainbow

Rígr, watcher, Heimdallr,
Of nine mothers you were born,
You bind the races of Gods and men,
Gjallarhorn at your lips.
Blow the horn when danger looms,
In spite of all the strength of Asgard,
Victory cannot be won.

Watchman of the Gods

Hail to Heimdallr!
Ever watching, ever ready,
Your keen eyes seeing far from Himinbjörg,
Where the Bifröst meets the sky.
But you are no stranger to travel;
You link the worlds of Gods and men,
As an ancestor to us all.
Friend of fair Frejya,
You retrieved the Brísingamen,
Triumphing over Odin's sworn brother,
Bravely fighting in seal form.
And you will fight him again,
Though this time not for a necklace,
But for your lives,
Which both of you shall forfeit,
On that bloody field of Vígríðr.
Master of the Gjallarhorn,
You are no stranger to fine mead,
And we honour you this night.
Hail Heimdallr!

The White God
-Keith Leggott

Hail to Heimdallr, the watcher!
Watcher of men, of the nine realms. The White God.
Father of men, of the three classes.
You visited Midgard,
Dined with couples and stayed over for the night,
Nine months later a class of people appeared,
With the birth of a son to each couple.
Heimdallr!
With vision so good you can see the wool on a sheep's back grow.
Keeper of the Gjallarhorn,
The sound of the calling of the Gods.
Guardian of the Gods.
Sometimes known as the golden God,
A God with golden teeth,
The son of nine mothers,
Owner of the horse Gulltopp.
Heimdallr!
We thank thee for keeping watch over the nine realms,
We thank thee for looking over the Gods,
And we thank thee for watching over Midgard!
We give this offering to you freely and with thanks.

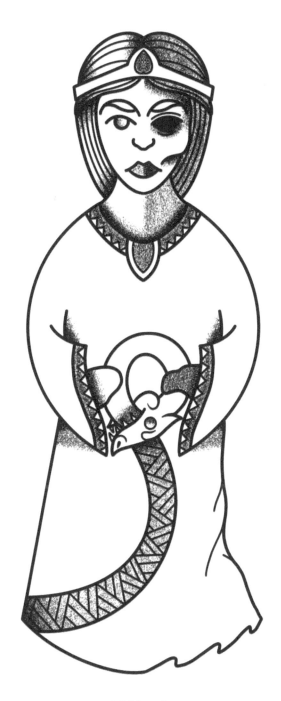

Hel

A Traveller Approaches

Hail to the mistress of Helheim!
Loki's daughter, hostess of the dead,
We call to you.
A traveller approaches.
They are tired, they are weary,
Their feet are sore.
They have travelled for many miles and many days,
On a journey few look forward to making.
They have toiled, they have laughed,
They have loved, they have cried.
They have suffered, they have cared,
They have lived, they have died.
They have crossed the Gjöll bridge,
And now they stand before Éljúðnir,
Before you, seeking your hospitality.
Please grant them sanctuary,
That they might be reunited with their ancestors.
Amongst their loving kin,
That they might rest now,
Free of life's trials and tribulations.
With food, and drink, and company,
That one day we too shall join them,
To share stories by the hearth fire.
Hail Hel!

Goddess of the Underworld

-Keith Leggott

Hel!
Goddess of the underworld, of Helheim.
Lady of darkness, daughter of Loki,
Goddess of the dead.
Banished by Odin to the world of the dead,
No longer allowed in our world of the living.
From you we learn how to make the most from a given situation.
We learn how no situation is a complete loss, a waste.
Hel!
Sister of the Fenris wolf and Jormungundr, the world serpent.
Half-sister to Sleipnir, Odin's great steed.
Half beauty and half rotten, grotesque monster.
Host of Baldur and wife after Loki's tricking of Hod.
Like your father you teach us patience.
You teach us how to wait for that which we desire,
As you wait for Ragnarok to gain vengeance,
Many, many years ahead.
We leave you this offering as thanks for all you have taught us.
But mainly Hel,
We give this offering freely to say thank you.

Host To The Dead
-Keith Leggott

To Hel,
Daughter to the God of mischief and trickery.
Queen of the realm of the underworld.
Queen of Helheim,
The land of those who have passed to the next part of their journey,
Whose realm is guarded by the great wolf-dog Garm,
And the river Gjöll.
To whom Odin sent Hermod to visit,
And ask for the return of Baldur and Nanna.
And who graciously gave a chance to Frigg;
If everything on earth agreed.
Hel, harsh on thieves and murderers,
Not so on those who lead a normal, decent life.
Host to those of us who die outside of battle,
Of illness, disability or old age.
Who waits patiently to be re-united with her father and her siblings.
Stoical, ever so serene and tranquil, waiting for a reunion;
Waiting for Ragnarok and revenge!
Hel, so much of your life is unknown to us.
So much we have yet to learn and we ask you for aide.
Show us the way to true patience as we seek to endure our ignorance,
As we continue our quest.
Accept our offering,
As our way of showing appreciation and gratitude for your lessons.
Accept our gift, given freely,
And accept our thanks.

The Hosts of the Dead

A Warm Place by the Fire

Hail to Hel, Lady of Helheim,
Your realm gives sanctuary, safety and security.
Hail to wise Odin and shining Freyja, hosts of the battle slain,
Who live well in your halls, preparing for one last battle.
Hail to beautiful Rán, host of those lost at sea,
In your hall beneath the waves, sailors are at peace.
We thank you all for hosting our ancestors in their life after death.
Giving them food and mead, and a warm place by the fire.
Wherever our fate takes us at the end of life's road,
We know that we shall reside with our ancestors,
Until the wolf breaks his chains.
Hail the hosts of the dead!

A Warrior Has Left Us

Odin, lord of Valhöll, Freyja, lady of Fölkvangr,
We call to you!
A warrior has left us, and joined your ranks.
There was a battle, here in Midgard,
The Valkyries came, and took our brave kinsman,
From our world to yours.
In life they fought to protect their family, their friends,
Their community.
Now they shall feast with you, fight with you, die beside you,
Each day, until the wolf breaks his bonds,
And they fight one final time,
On the field of Vígríðr.
May they serve you as faithfully as they have served us.
Hail Odin! Hail Freyja!

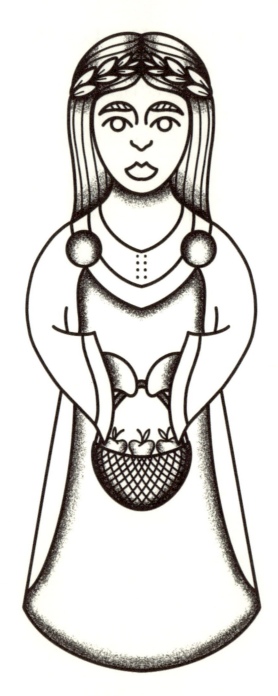

Idunna

Sustainer of the Gods

Hail to Idunna!
Sustainer of the Gods,
Without whom they would wither and die.
Beautiful maintainer of youth,
Whose golden apples are much sought after.
Acorn lady,
Led astray by the son of Laufrey,
But ultimately saved by the self-same trickster.
You preserve the Æsir and Vanir alike,
That they may preserve our world.
Hail Idunna!

Keeper of The Fruit
-Keith Leggott

Praise to Idunna!
Goddess of spring, Goddess of eternal youth and immortality.
Keeper and protector of the magical fruit,
Without which the Gods would age.
Wife of Bragi, God of poetry.
Praise to Idunna!
A victim of kidnapping by Loki and the giant Þjazi,
Who after being tricked by Loki was also rescued by Loki.
Who taught us hope as she never gave up hers.
Idunna, Goddess with the long golden-blonde hair.
Without whom, and without whose fruit,
The Gods began to show signs of ageing, signs of mortality.
Beloved by the whole assembly of Gods, their wives and offspring.
Though not the strongest of Asgard's inhabitants,
You show us the meaning of resolve,
Of earning the trust placed in you by others.
Praise to Idunna!
Though threatened by Þjazi with a number of atrocities,
You held firm.
Though threatened with your life you kept safe the fruit,
A heroic deed.
For this, Idunna, we thank you today.
We leave you this offering as a thank you for the traits you show,
And teach us.
Hail to Idunna!
A Goddess and a beauty with resolve, determination and grit.
Thank You!

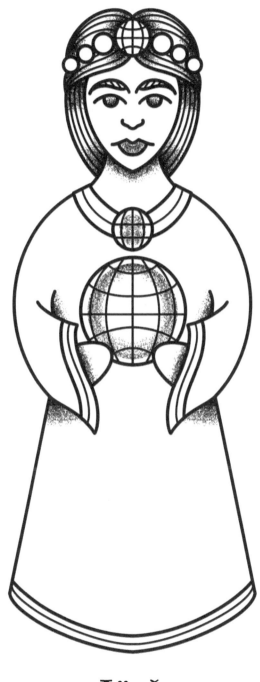

Jörð

Earth Mother

Hail to Jörð!
Earth mother,
All of the God's earthly gifts come through you.
Everything we offer them, you keep safe.
Daughter of night, sister of day,
Lover of Odin, mother of Thor.
You sustain us throughout our days,
Give us warmth, give us food, give us life.
Yet so often humankind don't appreciate you;
They pollute your rivers, and litter your fields.
They take, without giving back.
This must change. This must stop.
We must rediscover how to appreciate your gifts,
We must learn to take only enough,
As our ancestors did before us,
So that we may live in harmony.
Beautiful Jörð, bountiful Jörð,
Mother of us all.
Hail Jörð!

Hostess of the Living

Hail to Jörð!
Gracious hostess of the living,
Of birds, of animals, of mankind,
All owe their life to you,
For without you we would have no hearth.
Ancient lady,
Barer of Odin's most powerful son,
We owe you so much,
But all too often take you for granted.
Thank you for our homes,
Thank you for sustaining our lives,
And the lives of our kin.
Hail Jörð!

Jörð our Home

-Kristian Lewin-Petrov

Hail Jörð, mother of Thor,
Mother of us all and mother of the landvættir,
Giantess, first lover of Odin and most fertile of all the Vanir.
Hail Jörð, daughter of Nott and Anarr, giver and taker of lives.
Breasts that could drown a man,
Hips broad enough to spill forth triplets.
Hail Jörð, your beauty is loved by all who gaze upon you,
Your very touch causes trees to blossom and plants to grow,
Your wrath spawns exploding volcanoes,
And waves that sweep across Midgard.
Hail Jörð, for your presence provides us with all we need,
Goddess of all things not controllable by humans, of mountains,
Of trees, of rock and stone,
Hail Jörð, you give us love for the wild places,
The love of nature and the love of ourselves.
Hail Jörð!

Kvasir

Wisest of the Gods

Hail to Kvasir, wisest of the Gods!
Binder of Æsir and Vanir,
Their combined knowledge mixed at your very core.
None amongst Gods and men know more,
Of the way things are, or have been.
Great ancestor of poetry,
We thank you for your sacrifice.
Hail Kvasir!

Loki

Catalyst of Greatness

Hail to Loki!
Cunning one, master of the bright wolf of the hall.
Without whom we would sit back, fester, become weak.
Without whom we would not challenge ourselves,
To become the best that we can be.
Thor's companion,
The Alfather himself will take no ale prow,
Unless it is shared with his sworn brother.
Whilst at first your actions may seem harmful, spiteful, destructive,
You see further.
You are the catalyst of greatness.
You do that which the great Gods of Asgard cannot do,
You sacrifice your reputation for the greater good,
And for that we thank you.
Hail Loki!

Lord of Self-Sacrifice
- Keith Leggott

Hail to Loki!
The playful, the mischievous,
The trickster, the magician and the shape-shifter.
Companion and brother, son, lover, father and mother.
The one who keeps the Gods grounded,
Who will help the sons of Midgard,
Has hidden man from danger within the fire.
Loki, lord of self-sacrifice,
You have taught us to learn patience,
Especially with friends and those we call family.
You have shown us how to be humble and self-sacrificial,
As you saved Asgard's beauty,
And in doing so ultimately gave birth to Sleipnir.
At a social gathering you showed us all how to be brave.
To stand in front of many friends and tell many truths,
Only to be exiled.
Loki, you teach us to be a better person, a refined creature.
We honour you today Loki, for your dedication to friendship.
Through you, brother, we understand self-sacrifice.
We have the knowledge that to true friends and family,
We require nought in return.
Hail Loki! King of mischief, father of Fenrir, Hel,
Jormungundr and Narfi,
We leave you this offering with free will and thanks.

Trickster & Adventurer
- Keith Leggott

Hail to Loki!
Trickster, traveller and travelling companion,
Searcher of adventure.
Loki; maid of honour for the return of Mjölnir.
Who lost narrowly to fire itself, in the shape of Logi,
In a famous eating contest in Utgard.
Who hid the peasants' son inside the flames,
To protect him from a Giant.
Loki, son of giants – God in Asgard.
Aide to some and hindrance to others.
Bird, mare, salmon and old woman,
You have been all of these, to either help, evade or hinder others.
We acknowledge your ability to change for each situation.
Son of Farbauti, cruel striker, and Laufey,
Mate of Angrboda, anguish boding,
Husband of Sigyn, friend of victory,
Father of Hel, Jormungandr, Fenrir, Narfi and Nari.
Mother of Sleipnir, the son of Svadilfari.
The cause of the giant Þjazi's death,
And thus the appearance of Skaði in Asgard.
We leave you this offering with thanks.

Shaver of the Golden Hair

-Keith Leggott

To Loki, brother of Helbindi and Byleistr, blood brother of Odin.
The trickster who played with mistletoe,
Who took Idunna for a walk outside of Asgard,
The Gods ageing until her return.
Who killed an otter that was human, but paid his dues in gold.
Praise to Loki, who travelled with Thor,
Both dressed as women, to retrieve Mjölnir.
Who made Skaði laugh as she entered Asgard,
Looking for revenge for the death of her father.
Who shaved Sif's head of her beautiful hair,
But replaced it with magically spun gold.
Who returned with gifts for Odin, Thor, Sif and Freyr.
Bringing Draupnir, the magic golden arm-ring,
Mjölnir, Thor's hammer,
And the magic ship named Skidbladnir.
Hail to Loki! Son of a giant, lover of a giantess,
Father of three children banished from Asgard.
Who saved his own head by saving his neck,
To the cheers of other Gods.
Who spared the Gods from giving up Freyja to be a giant's wife.
Who by doing this became pregnant with Sleipnir.
Loki, we leave you this offering with thanks, of free will,
And we hope that it pleases you.

Misunderstood by the Majority
-Keith Leggott

Hail to Loki!
Born a giant, welcomed to Asgard, blood brother of Odin.
A playful character and truly a mischievous soul.
At times merely impish,
A childlike prankster with harmless shenanigans,
Easily and quickly rectified.
Though also malicious, and venomous, and at times vengeful.
You make it hard for us to love you.
Extremely difficult to trust you.
Though you also do good for man when we requires it.
Loki, misunderstood by the majority, hastily blamed by many.
We acknowledge your pain,
Your reasons and your need for vengeance and disruption.
As you were summoned to Asgard by your blood brother Odin,
Your children were taken from you, and either banished or chained.
You had already presented one child, Sleipnir,
To the Alfather, and now lost a further three.
Loki, we understand your anguish,
And your desire to cause some pain to those responsible.
A desire that we in Midgard not only recognise,
But actually partake of.
We leave this offering to you as a token of love and respect.
We leave this offering as a thank you for lessons learned,
For teaching us that life can indeed continue,
After such a disruptive and devastating loss.
We leave you this offering with hope that it pleases you.
We leave this offering of our own free will.

Mani

Celestial Guide

Hail to Mani, the light in the darkness!
Waxer, waner, shiner, gleamer,
Counter of the days,
You guide us whilst your sister sleeps.
You guide the sailor and the magician alike.
You guide our lives.
Lover of the giantess, bringer of tides,
We thank you this night.
Hail Mani!

A Familiar Face

Hail Mani!
We call to you, oh light in the darkness.
We may travel far from home,
To strange, unfamiliar places;
Places where we know not a soul,
With strange flora and fauna,
Unknown wights, and even unknown Gods.
Yet your familiar face will always be there on a clear night.
No matter how far we travel, you are with us, Mani,
To guide us, to comfort us,
With a welcome reminder of home far away.
We know that whilst you look down on us,
Wherever we are,
You are also looking over our kin.
We look to the sky, and see the same face:
Your face.
Hail Mani!

Njörð

Lord of Nóatún

To the Lord of Nóatún, Hail!
Elder Van, master of the shore,
Who loves Þjazi's daughter in vain.
Friend of the merchant and the fisherman,
Bringer of wealth,
You came to Asgard as a hostage,
But stayed as a friend.
Father of prosperous Freyr,
And shining Freyja,
You protect those who tread the wave road.
Hail Njörð!

Sharer of Wealth

Hail Njörð!
Ruler of the high-timbered temple,
Lover of the songs of swans,
To you we give thanks for the sea's bounty.
For sharing with us the salmon,
The sea bass, the squid.
These gifts sustain us,
But we must be careful to take only our fair share,
And not damage your beautiful realm in the process.
Sharer of wealth,
For whom the wolf-song is hateful,
Yours is the boundary,
Where the sea meets the shore,
Neither one world nor another.
Hail Njörð!

Protector of the Boundary

Hail Njörð!
Generous master of the shore,
We feel your presence where earth and water meet.
A troubled relationship, a destructive relationship,
But a relationship with so much to give.
Nourishment, trade, amusement, relaxation,
All these you facilitate, all these you share.
Our island people owe much to our shore, to you.
Britannia may have ruled the waves,
But it was you, Njörð,
Who gave her the gifts with which to rule.
Sharer of the ocean's bounty,
Protector of the boundary,
We honour you this day.
Hail Njörð!

The Norns

A Turn of Your Spindle

Hail to Urðr, hail to Verðandi, hail to Skuld,
Hail to the Norns!
Ancient spinners, with our fates in your hands.
Spinning, weaving, cutting,
The web of wyrd is your great creation.
Every chance encounter, every turn of fate,
Every win, every loss,
All are but a turn of your spindle,
A stitch of your needle,
A cut of your shears.
Hail the Norns!

At the Roots of the World Tree

Hail to the Norns!
Ancient weavers at the roots of the world tree,
With runes you pass your magic to the nine worlds,
With sacred threads you spin our wyrd.
Our past, our present and our future;
All are caught up in the web.
Every encounter, with human, animal, wight or God,
Every event in our lives,
Nothing happens in isolation,
And you oversee it all.
Sustaining Yggdrasil, sustaining our destiny,
Deciding when our journey will end;
All this you do,
And we thank you.
Hail the Norns!

The Gods' Own County

Odin

Wise One of Many Names

Hail to Biflindi, to Grímnir, to Forni,
Hail to Draugadróttinn, to Gapþrosnir, to Hildolfr,
Hail to Hangadróttinn, to Hrafnáss, to Sigtryggr,
Hail to Hávi, to Jafnhárr, to Þriði,
Hail to Skollvaldr, to Viðurr to Yggr,
Hail to Odin!
Wise one of many names, we honour you this night!
Stalker of the standard-road,
You gather the wolf-feeders to your hall.
Endless seeker of knowledge,
You hung from the windy tree,
So that you may take up the runes.
Friend of Jarls,
From Hlidskjalf you rule over the Gods of Asgard.
Lord of Valhöll,
Geri and Freki guard your gates.
Far wonderer,
Huginn and Muninn tell you of the deeds of men.
Far sighted one,
Not afraid to do what needs to be done.
Sworn brother of Loki,
You will not take the cauldron liquid without him.
Ancient One, Mighty One, Terrible One,
Alfather.
Hail Odin!

Lord of War

Odin, Lord of War, leader of the Einherjar,
Master of Valhalla, we call to you! Wise one,
Whose Valkyries choose those who will fight alongside you at
Ragnarok.
You who knows sacrifice,
And is not afraid to do that which may seem wrong,
In order to achieve the ultimate goal.
We honour you.
Hail Odin!

Lord of the Long Night

To the lord of the long night hail!
Sleipnir's rider, you tear across the sky, with the hunt in tow,
Bringing death to the old year, making way for the life of the new.
This Yule night we thank you for the gift of the runes,
The knowledge that you sacrificed so much for,
Hanging for nine days from the windy tree.
God of madness, we honour you as we gather with our family,
On this longest and darkest of nights.
Hail Odin!

Facing the Enemy Within

Alfather,
You who have seen what is to be,
And know what must be done.
You who must fight the enemy within,
As well as the great foes of Asgard.
Burdened by the weight of fates you cannot control,
Weighed down by the regret of your actions,
Even though they were ultimately right.
Most high, nobody can truly understand,
Not even your fellow Gods can help shoulder the burden,
That the knowledge has brought upon you.
Yet you do not give up,
You show us how to remain strong,
To fight, when our own minds betray us.
Taking strength in the knowledge that kith and kin depend on you,
You don't give up, as to do so would be to fail the world.
Whilst nobody can take the burden from you,
They can stand with you, comfort you,
As our friends and family can support us,
Through all of life's hardships.
God of madness,
We thank you for your example,
We thank you for your many sacrifices,
And we thank you for giving us strength.
For our families, for ourselves, and for you.
Hail Odin!

Son of Bor

-Keith Leggott

Hail to Odin!
Alfather, father of the Gods, father of Thor.
A frequent visitor to our world of Midgard,
A frequent traveller throughout this realm.
We learn from you so many things.
Odin, friend, blood brother and travelling companion of Loki.
Son of Bor, brother of Villi and Ve.
With brothers you created the universe,
Created Midgard and original man.
Giving life to Ask and Embla.
Odin, Who hung himself from Yggdrasil, the world tree,
For a whole nine days to learn the secret of the runes.
Speared by Gungnir to sacrifice yourself to yourself.
By doing this you taught us the importance of knowledge,
Of wisdom.
With your ravens Huginn, thought, and Muninn, memory,
Bringing news, you remain all knowledgeable.
As the wolves Geri, ravener, and Freki, greed,
Sit at your feet, you look down upon our world.
Watching.
We thank you Alfather for keeping watch over us.
We leave you this offering as a thank you for your teachings.
Hail to Odin, God of war, God of poetry.
Hail Odin, The Alfather!

Lord of Valhalla

-Keith Leggott

Odin, Alfather Owner of Draupnir, the magic golden ring.
Father of Vidar and Vali, survivors of Ragnarok.
A God who willingly sacrificed one of his eyes for knowledge.
Rewarded with a drink from Mimir's well.
Who with his brothers built the universe from Ymir.
Hail to Odin; sustaining himself with wine alone,
And the occasional apple from Idunna.
Who rides Sleipnir, offspring of Loki, and fastest of all steeds.
Who banished Hel, daughter of Loki,
To the realm of the same name,
To become Queen and ruler of the dead.
Who had Loki's son Jormungundr, the Midgard serpent,
Into the ocean to grow,
And who had Loki's greatest child, Fenris, bound and restrained.
Hail To Odin;
Who tricked Gunnlod into allowing him to drink from
Kvasir's mead.
Ruler of the Great Hall, Valhöll,
With its 540 rooms, where warriors live, fight and party,
Eating from Sooty Black,
The boar with a never-ending supply of meat.
We leave this offering as thanks to the Alfather,
We offer these things freely,
With hopes that they please the father of the Gods.

Rán

Queen of the Deep

Hail to fair Rán, Queen of the deep.
Rightfully feared by those who tread your road,
For the sea deserves their respect.
Taker of sailors,
Even the most prepared can find themselves in your net.
Gracious host of those who find your favour,
In your legendary hall beneath the waves.
Your jealousy is well known,
Yet tales of your beauty precede you.
Wife of Ægir, mother of waves, hostess of the Gods,
So often misunderstood.
Hail Rán!

We Journey to Your Realm

Gracious Rán, lady of the deep, we call to you!
We will soon journey deep into your realm,
And ask that you grant us safe passage.
Guide us in the darkness,
Give us warmth in the cold,
As you have seen fit to do in past.
We honour you, oh beautiful Goddess.
We offer you gold.
We hope to merely pass through your hall,
But should the Norns decide we should stay,
We can take comfort in the tales of your hospitality.
Hail Rán!

Giving Thanks for Safe Passage

To the Queen of deep, hail!
We have walked your road,
And have returned unscathed.
We thank you for accepting our offerings,
And watching over us,
Letting us pass safely through your realm,
For only the fool takes this for granted.
The ocean seems interminable to men,
If they venture on the rolling bark,
And the waves of the sea terrify them.
And yet your waters give us so much,
Should we gain your blessing.
Sustenance, transport, livelihood.
Protection from our foes,
A place from which to strike unexpectedly,
At those who would do harm to our kin.
As we leave your realm once again,
And return to the land,
To be once more amongst our kin,
We thank you wholeheartedly for preserving us.
Hail Rán!

A Kinsman at Your Door

We call to the great hostess of the deep.
A kinsman has left us, and come to your door,
Seeking your protecting, your hospitality, and a seat in your hall.
They have walked the roads of men for the last time,
They have set sail, never to return to our hearth,
But instead to be with all those sailors,
Whose threads where cut amongst the roiling waves,
And found themselves at your mercy.
We make offering to you this day,
As they made offerings to you,
And ask that you take in our beloved kin,
Our seafarer, who knew your road well.
Born of a land they left behind,
Loved by a kin they sailed to protect.
In death they are with you,
For when they lived, they chose the sea.
Hail Rán!

Seaxnēat

You Guide Our Tribe
-Tara Skinner

Hail Seaxnēat!
God of family, kin and companionship,
From your white horse, you guide our tribe,
Through the world tree Yggdrasil, to which we ascribe.
Sword in hand, you help our family navigate the trials of this land.
Son of Woden, protector of our tribe and hearth,
We call you. Hail Seaxnēat!

Your People Will Not Forget You

Hail to Seaxnēat!
Helper of the Saxons,
Sword God, ancestor of kings.
We embrace your deeds and words,
Though so much of your wisdom has been stolen from us,
By those who would have us forget you.
But your people will not forget you.
You rode with them across the cold North Sea,
To a new and mysterious land,
And stood with them in battle,
That they might hold that land against all foes.
You helped them to raise their families,
And strengthened their bonds of kinship.
You helped them raise their livestock and grow their crops,
That they might live in peace and prosperity.
We are those people, your people,
And your people will not forget you.
Hail Seaxnēat!

Sif

Rowan Lady

Hail to golden haired Sif!
Wife of the Thunderer,
Patient one, who showed restraint,
In the face of the trickster's taunts,
Even after he took your scalp cords.
Lady of the golden hair, loveliest of women,
You bring wheat to our fields,
That we might have bread and ale,
For the cold winter nights.
Rowan Lady,
You bless our marriages, our families, our children.
Hail Sif!

Goddess Of The Harvest Hair
-Keith Leggott

Hail to Sif, wife of Thor,
Goddess with the golden hair.
Harvest hair so beloved by Thor and stolen by Loki.
Because of your husband's love and anger,
Loki got you the magical golden hair and Thor his hammer Mjölnir.
Sif, we thank you for being such a dutiful,
Loving and supporting wife.
We thank you for the family atmosphere you give,
To the protector of Asgard and Midgard.
We are grateful for the patience you show,
When your husband disappears on his travels,
And the soothing environment when he returns.
Sif, Goddess of the harvest, mother of Ullr, wife of Thor.
A Goddess of the earth united in marriage to a God of the sky.
We thank you for all you are and all you do.
Beautiful and strong, caring and giving.
Sif, we leave you this offering as a thank you,
As a symbol of our respect.
We hope it pleases you,
And is accepted in the same spirit with which it is freely given.

Skaði

Þjazi's Brave Daughter

Hail to Skaði, Lady of the mountains!
Þjazi's brave daughter,
You showed no fear when you travelled to Asgard,
To avenge your father.
Your demands were met,
You left with your family's honour restored.
Njörð's strong bride,
Your love is a troubled one.
You find no rest beside the shore,
He no peace amongst the ice.
Sleep you could not on the sea beds,
for the screeching of the bird.
Hateful for him are the mountains.
Ski-Goddess, protector of travellers,
Mother of many sons.
We honour you this day.
Hail Skaði!

Bringer of Warmth to Our Hearts

To the Goddess of winter, hail!
Goddess of the mountain, Goddess of snow,
Travelling by ski, hunting with bow,
Fighter for justice, for laughter, for love,
Your father's bright eyes, shining above.
Chooser of feet, amused by the goat,
Placer of serpent, above Loki's throat,
Bringing of warmth to our hearts, on cold winter nights,
Giving the strength, to fight for what's right.
Your family broken, your spouse far away,
You know true hardship, in every way.
But you don't sit and ponder, on what might have been,
You ski and you hunt, with eyes bright and keen,
Strong as the mountain, cold as the snow,
We know you each time, the icy winds blow.
Hail Skaði!

Giantess From the Cold
-Keith Leggott

Skaði!
A giantess coming in from the cold,
Married to the God of the sea.
We ask for your protection,
Using your considerable strength.
A Queen of the hunt and fierce with a bow,
Your love of the cold rings true to us in the north.
Skaði, our giant Goddess from the high mountains.
You teach us patience, you teach us forgiveness.
You teach us diplomacy and how to deal with disappointment.
Skaði, you have shown us the strength to stand up for ourselves.
Taught us how to demand retribution,
Yet also how to refrain from personal revenge.
Skaði, daughter of Þjazi the giant,
The Goddess, the Queen, thou art large and thou art fierce.
You stand tall, you stand Strong,
You stand against injustice.
We give thanks to your being,
And we leave this offering freely,
In thanks.

Wife of Njörð

-Keith Leggott

Strong, proud, determined and fearless daughter of Þjazi.
Unafraid to march alone into Asgard,
The domain of the Gods: the enemy.
Set upon retribution for the death of a father.
Unflinching in your determination for justice and revenge;
Until tricked by Loki.
We learn from you the act of courage,
Self-determination and fearlessness.
Skaði,
Adopted into the family of Asgard,
Though truly a giant you are now also a Goddess.
After your marriage to Njörð,
Sealing the peace between yourself and Asgard,
Came to an end,
You show us your strength of will,
And ability to live an almost solitary life in the mountains.
You show us patience and vengeance,
As you finally gain revenge on Loki,
By placing the venom-dripping snake above his bound body.
You teach us that mountain ranges can be loved and appreciated,
Just as much as the forest.
Skaði, we thank you for everything you have shown us.
How to appreciate outside of the norm.
We thank you for teaching us patience, forgiveness and tactfulness.
We thank you for coming to Asgard and becoming part of the family.
And we leave you this offering as a thank you.
To you, Skaði, may you enjoy this offering and continue to teach us,
As you wait to fight with the Gods at Ragnarok.

Sunna

Lady of Light, Lady of Life

Hail to Sunna!
Lady of light, lady of life!
Without your warming rays there would be nothing but darkness.
No life, no laughter, no love.
On long summer days we bask in your warm embrace,
On cold winter's afternoons we take comfort,
As we glimpse your face through the clouds.
Mani's sister, ever glowing day star,
May Arvakr and Alsviðr keep you ahead of the wolf.
Hail Sunna!

A Glimpse of Your Face

Sunna!
Shining lady, bringer of life.
In the depths of winter the nights are long, cold and dark.
We gather by the fire, pulling blankets around us,
We long for your return.
We dream of the long, warm days,
Days where you will nourish us,
Days that seem so far away,
As we fight the winter frosts.
We glimpse your face between the clouds,
And take heart in your short time with us each day,
Knowing that you will return,
In all your glory, radiance and beauty.
Hail Sunna!

Thor

Friend to the Sons & Daughters of the Earth

Hail to mighty Thor!
Friend to all sons and daughters of the earth,
Foe to the children of Þorn.
Mjölnir's wielder,
Your winds guide the shield provider of the warships prow;
Your rains bring life to the field;
Your high flames light the sky.
Serpent's bane,
You empty more ale-prows than all the kin of Ingvi-Freyr;
You travel far with the wolf's father;
You protect the realms of Gods and men.
Thunderer! Warder! Protector!
We call to you!
Hail Thor!

Protector of Gods and Men

We call to the thunderer!
We call to the warder!
We call to Thor!
Strongest of the Gods we call to you,
Great protector of Gods and men alike.
With the hammer of the Gods in your hand,
You protect the boundaries of Asgard and Midgard,
From giant, from giantess, from serpent.
Drainer of oceans, lifter of Jörmungandr,
You who fought bravely against the ravages of age,
Champion of Asgard, your strength is unmatched,
Your bravery legendary, your loyalty unquestionable.
We thank you for your protection, oh lightning bringer,
We thank you for inspiring our own strength in all that we do.
Hail Thor!

A Prayer to Thor
-Daniel Warden

Hail to Thor!
Hammer-wielder! Lightening-Rider!
Hail to he who brings us strength and courage,
On the lonely roads of life.
May you inspire us to be courageous, to be brave and strong!
May we think of you every time the thunder rolls,
Or lightning flashes across the stormy sky!
May we smile at storm-time for we know you are with us Thor!
When red sky's smile let us know it is your red beard,
Blown by the winds!
Hail to you Thor, smasher of giants!
Hail to you Thor, strongest of Gods!
And may you forever protect us!

Protector of Man and Asgard
-Keith Leggott

Hail Thor!
Protector of the Gods and of Asgard,
Protector of men and their home of Midgard.
Traveller, wanderer, seeker of justice.
Destroyer of Jotunns, searcher for the Midgard serpent.
Son of the Alfather, strongest of all the Gods.
Thor, worthy of wielding Mjölnir,
Enabling the destruction of numerous giants.
Husband of Sif, Goddess with the beautiful golden hair.
Travelling companion of Loki, the blood brother.
Sometimes quick to anger,
Especially when concerning Jotunns or Loki.
Wearer of the great belt of strength, Megingjord,
And of Jarngreipr, the iron gloves that help wield Mjölnir.
Hail to Thor: The red-haired and red-bearded God of thunder,
And God of lightning.
Lover of Jarnsaxa, one Jotunn Thor will not destroy with Mjölnir.
With Jarnsaxa, you begat Magni – a survivor of Ragnarok.
Hail to Thor, God, warrior and protector.
We leave you this offering as a thank you,
We leave you this offering freely and with the greatest of intentions.
We thank you Thor, and hope this offering pleases you.

Wielder of Mjölnir
-Keith Leggott

Hail to Thor!
Riding in his chariot,
Pulled by the Goats Tanngrisnir and Tanngnjostr.
Son of Odin, the Alfather.
Scariest, angriest and strongest of the Gods.
Traveller and adventurer, fighter and friend.
Hail to Thor!
Father, brother, husband, lover, friend and destroyer.
Son and nephew of the creatures of the universe.
Commander of the elements; of thunder, of lightening.
Capable of devouring a couple of bulls at a feast.
Whose appetite for mead, the nectar of the Gods, is insatiable.
Hail to Thor!
Who wrestled against time and old age,
Whose strength was tested,
As he managed to partially lift Jormungandr.
Whose draught from the mead cup in Utgard,
Lowered sea levels and gave us the waves.
Wielder of Mjölnir, protector of Asgard,
A favourite amongst the men of Midgard.
We leave you this offering with free will,
In the hope that it pleases you.

The Companions of Thor

Hail to the companions of Thor!
As the mighty thunderer rides across the sky,
Fiery in both look and temperament,
Protecting Gods and men from the chaos,
We remember you, his companions.
We thank you for the support you give him,
So that he can continue to protect us.
We thank the goats, Snarler and Grinder,
For pulling the loud riders chariot,
And providing him with sustenance.
We thank Þjálfi and Röskva,
For your dedication to serving your master.
We thank Thor's travelling companion,
The trickster, whose devious skills compliment Asa-Thor's strength,
And help him to overcome his foes.
We thank Sif, his bride, and Jarnsaxa, mother of his children,
And we honour Mjölnir, hammer of the Gods,
The mighty weapon with which the hallower protects us.
Hail the companions of Thor!

Fair Winds & Following Seas

Hail Thor!
A fisherman's friend, a sailor's guide,
Giving fair winds and following seas to those who earn your favour.
You are no stranger to the storm-twisted enclosure of man;
From Hymir's boat you stalked the serpent.
From Utgard-Loki's horn you drank deeply,
So deeply that you gave us the tides,
As the seas rose and fell with each great draught.
Your greatest foe dwells in the land of salmon,
Yet the cod is yours.
Thunderer! Those who disrespect you risk your wrath.
As you bring the great storm to the plain of Ægir,
Tearing the sail-yard feather, smashing the sea feet,
And sending the wave horse and her riders to face Rán's judgement.
Not always foremost amongst the Gods associated with the waves,
Only the naïve would neglect you before treading the prow road.
Hail the Thunderer! Hail the serpent's bane! Hail Thor!

Lord of Bilskirnir
-Keith Leggott

Thor!
The red-headed God of thunder and farm crops.
Lord of the hall named Bilskirnir,
So large it contains some five-hundred and forty doors.
Owner of the goats Tooth-Grinder and Tooth-Gnasher,
Which can be killed to provide a feast at night,
And that shall be reborn, ready for transport upon the morn!
Thor!
Favoured among the men of Midgard,
Whom you protect from harm.
Son of Odin and Jörð,
With a strength unmatched.
You teach us of courage, of bravery,
As you fight continuously against the Jotunns.
We learn from you the importance of family, of friends,
Of kin, and the desire to protect them.
We also learn of self-sacrifice,
As you battle the world-serpent at Ragnarok;
Taking your final nine steps after eventually slaying the monster:
Son of Loki, your friend.
This final act of bravery shows the people of Midgard that patience,
Perseverance, determination and tenacity,
Are not only important but required traits for success.
Thor!
We leave you this offering of our own free-will,
And hope you will accept both it and our thanks.
We thank you for your protection and for the lessons you teach us.
We leave this offering as a gesture of thanks,
For your continued teachings and protection.
Hail Thor! God, warrior, son, brother, fighter, husband, lover,
Protector. Son of Odin, grandson of Bor.

Tyr

Friend of the Wolf

Hail to Tyr!
Lord of the thing, lord of justice, prince of temples.
Ancient warrior,
Yours is the sword storm for what is right.
You know the true pain of sacrifice,
And show us the true value of an oath.
Friend of the wolf,
You did what needed to be done;
Losing your hand, but keeping your honour,
Showing us the true value of reputation.
Upholder of law,
You will not rest until justice is served,
Vengeance gained, frith restored.
We know so little of your deeds,
Yet you are a shining example to us all.
Hail Tyr!

Most Honourable of the Æsir

Hail the Tyr!
Called one hand, and leavings of the wolf.
But you are a God of justice, of strength, of war.
Your name a battle-cry across the ages,
Your rune a symbol of strength.
You protect the soldier on the battlefield,
You give courage to those seeking recompense.
You know sacrifice.
You know pain.
You know that an oath cannot be broken,
No matter the cost.
You knew your days on the killing field were over,
When you placed your sword arm in the wolf bite,
But you knew what must be done.
Just one, brave one, noble one,
Most honourable of the Æsir,
Hail Tyr!

The Disabled Warrior
-Keith Leggott

Tyr!
The God who proved his bravery,
To ensure the safety of Asgard's residents.
You willingly gave your right hand to ensnare the Fenris wolf!
Because of you the Gods were able to place Gleipnir,
The magical fetter, upon the wolf.
You have shown us how to overcome a disability,
Taught us the importance of family, of friends.
Tyr, a fighter, a leader, a disabled warrior,
A favourite amongst the Gods,
God of war, and God of justice.
So important to the inhabitants of Midgard,
that we named a day of the week after you.
Hail to Tyr, Son of Hymir, an angry jotun,
And grandson of a hateful nine hundred headed female beast.
We praise your loyalty and bravery,
We leave for you this offering as a gift,
We leave for you this offering as a thank you.
Hail to the god of bravery,
Hail to the God of war!

Ullr

Dweller of the Yew Dale

Hail to Ullr!
Dweller of the yew dale, God of the shield, master of the hunt.
We know so few of your tales, yet we know you were revered.
Beautiful son of Sif, you guide the winter traveller,
Across sea and snow, as you travelled with the magic bone.
Glorious one, master of single combat,
You guide our hand in the duel.
Winter God,
The long dark nights are yours.
Hail Ullr!

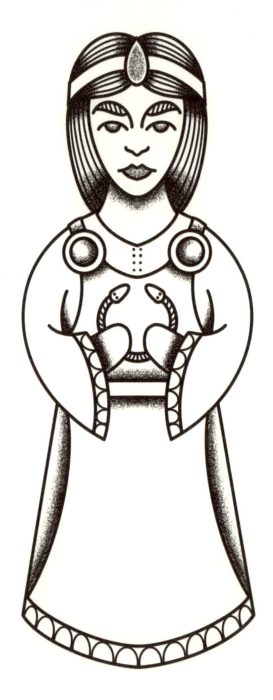

Var

An Oath Sworn

Hail to Var!
Honest Goddess, witness the oaths we swear here today.
Truthful Goddess, bless all those who keep their word.
Honourable Goddess, bring vengeance upon the untrustworthy.
Var, you listen carefully to all oaths spoken,
Remembering the details, ensuring they are upheld.
Friend to those who stand firmly by their pledge,
Punisher of the liar and the double crosser,
You guide us in upholding our honourable reputations.
Hail Var!

Vidar

God of Vengeance

We call to the God of vengeance!
Enemy and slayer of Fenris wolf,
You show us that transgressions cannot go unpunished,
That family honour most be upheld,
No matter the danger, no matter the cost.
Wearer of the thick shoe, survivor of the flames, Silent As,
You whose strength so nearly matches that of your brother Thor.
Brave one, reliable one, Odin's avenging son,
We honour you.
Hail Vidar!

After the Destruction and the Flame

Hail to Vidar!
The silent God,
You who will survive the great storm of swords,
In which you will slay the trickster's lupine son,
Avenging the Alfather's death.
You who will take your father's seat,
And rule Asgard in his stead,
As Magni and Modi take up Mjölnir,
And Lif and Lifthrasir emerge from Hoddmimisholt,
To repopulate the realms of men.
After the destruction and the flame,
You will rule as the cycle starts again.
Hail Vidar!

The Wights

The Waterwights

Hail to the näck, the nöck and the nixie,
Hail to the nykkur, the marbendill, the haffrú,
Hail to the Sjorå, the seal folk, the draug.
Hail to the waterwights!
In lakes and rivers, shores and seas,
You haunt the murky depths.
You prey on the unwitting man,
Who doesn't watch his step.
Calling sailors to the rocks,
Or dragging them below,
It's not even unheard of,
For you to deal the deadly blow.
Yet some of you are friendly,
Even human at Twelfth Night.
And whilst we must be wary,
With a gift you'll do us right.
Hail the waterwights!

An Unfamiliar Place

Hail to the wights of this unfamiliar place.
You do not know us, and we do not know you.
We have travelled to your lands in peace,
And mean you no harm.
We shall endeavour to do no damage to your home,
We shall not steal from you,
We shall leave your lands as we found them.
We ask that you do us no harm,
We ask that you do not take from us,
We ask that you let us leave in peace.
Hail the Wights!

Guests in Your Home

We call to the wights, the spirits, the hidden folk,
And all who inhabit this space.
The spirits of the land, the trees, the water, the air.
We are but guests in your home,
And we thank you for sharing it with us this night.
We thank you for sharing the fruits of the land, it's beauty, it's peace.
And we promise to respect your home,
Leaving it as we found it when we depart.
Hail the spirits of the land!

The Housewights

Hail to the wights of our home!
Spirits who were here before us, and will remain when we have gone.
This is our home, but it is also your home,
We share it with you as equals, and as friends.
We ask that you help us in our endeavours,
Guiding the yeast when we bake and brew,
Watching over our family, helping us to keep them safe.
In return we shall honour you,
We shall respect your space, and make you offerings,
Sharing what we have with you, as you share your home.
Hail the housewights!

Wights of the Tavern

Hail to the wights of the tavern!
Welcoming spirits, who lift our spirits, as we quaff spirits!
You inhabit this space of mirth,
Where we gather at the end of a long days toil,
To rest our weary bones,
And drink our fill in good company.
Be it the Dodger, the Swan, the King's Arms,
In the tavern we find warmth, we find sanctity,
We find hospitality.
As we eat and drink, putting the worries of the world to one side,
We thank you for sharing your space with us,
And letting us leave in peace, if a little worse for wear!
Hail the wights of the tavern!

Wights of the North

We call upon the landvættir, wights of this place,
And upon Brigantia, ancient lady of the north.
We thank you for sharing your home with us this day.
We also honour the water wights,
Who live in our rivers and surround our island,
Protecting our seafarers.
Hail the wights!

The Ancestors

The Disir

Hail to the Disir!
Ancient women, grandmothers, mothers.
You brought life to our ancestors, and to us.
You raised us, either in your own life time,
Or through your spiritual guidance.
You helped us grow, to become who we are today.
Now we are grown, you continue to help us,
In all matters of the family.
Through your strength you guide us,
Helping us to raise future generations.
We thank you for the gift of life,
For without you we could not be.
Hail the Disir!

The Alfar

Hail to the Alfar!
Residing together, family reunited in death.
You dwell amongst the spirits of the land.
We keep your tales alive,
So that one day you may welcome us,
With a horn of mead beside the hearth.
Hail the Alfar!

The Einherjar

To the Einherjar, and all those lost in war, Hail!
You who made the ultimate sacrifice, in defence of those you loved.
Those who faced the true horrors of war,
So that we may live in peace.
Whether warriors, or civilians caught in battle,
We honour your sacrifice.
We ask that you guide all those who protect the vulnerable,
Protect frith, protect peace.
We ask that you give us the strength to follow your example,
Should it be required of us,
So that our families and our communities may live on.
Hail!

Our Ever-Present Guides

We call to the ancestors.
Those who have come before us,
Who continue to guide us to become the best we can be.
Whether as warriors, as farmers, as mothers,
Whatever your trade, your deeds,
You not only provide us with an example,
But you continue to actively guide us in our lives,
Watching over your descendants as your own children.
We are the product of your loves and your lives,
And we shall do our utmost to uphold your honour and reputations.
Hail the ancestors!

Military Prayers

Naval Prayer

Odin, Skyfather, lord of war, who rules over Asgard;
Ægir, father of the waves; Rán, gracious host of those lost at sea;
Njörð, who rules where the sea meets the shore; mighty Thor,
Master of tides until the wolf breaks his bonds, Hail!
We honour you with word and deed,
And ask you to bless the fleet in which we serve.
Preserve us from the dangers of the sea,
And grant us the strength to overcome the violence of the enemy;
That we may be a safeguard unto our most gracious Sovereign Lady,
Queen Elizabeth, and her dominions,
And a security for such as pass on the seas,
Upon their lawful occasions;
That the inhabitants of our island may in frith honour our Gods;
And that we may return victorious to enjoy the blessings of the land,
With the fruits of our labours;
And with a thankful remembrance of thy blessings,
To honour our Gods, wights and ancestors. Hail!

A Soldier's Prayer

I am going to war,
Leaving loved ones behind.
I am leaving what is precious,
But I´m not going alone.
The Gods are with me,
In all the dark places.

Æsir, ease their hearts,
When my people miss me.
Æsir, stand with me,
When I am facing death.
Æsir, look after my loved ones,
As I would.

Royal Marines Prayer

Æsir! Vanir!
Who through many generations have united and inspired the members of our Corps,
Grant your blessings on Royal Marines serving across Midgard.
Look favourably upon all our efforts and endeavours,
And may our laurels be those of gallantry and honour,
Loyalty and courage.
We ask these things in the name of the Gods,
The wights and the ancestors.
Hail!

Submariner's Prayer

Æsir, Vanir, we call to thee,
for all submariners,
Beneath the sea.

In depths of oceans, as oft we stray,
So far from night, so far from day,
We would ask you guide our strength to grow,
To face the perils down below.

Odin grant us strength of mind,
That 'ere the darkness wont us blind,
We seek protection from the deep,
Freyr grant us peace when 'ere we sleep.

Of hearth and kindred far away,
We ask Frigg's care for them each day,
Until we surface once again,
To drink Jörð's air, and feel Thor's rain.

We ask your guiding light to show,
A safe progression sure and slow,
Hail Ægir, Rán, Wights of the sea,
From we submariners,
Beneath the Sea.

Resurgam.

Air Force Prayer

Mighty Thor!
Who tears through the clouds in your chariot,
And with Mjölnir brings the storm,
Look with favour upon the Royal Air Force.
Make us a tower of strength to our Queen and to our country.
Help us to do our duty with prudence and with fearlessness,
Confident that in life or in death we will protect our kin.
Grant this in the name of the Gods.
Hail!

Songs & Poems

Thank the Gods it's Yule

Here we're all gathered around the hearth fire,
To drink and be merry, fulfilling desires,
Oh to be surrounded with brave men on all fronts,
But we'll have to make do 'cos we're stuck with you...

Bring me more meat and bring me more mead!
We'll tell tall tales and boast of our deeds!
We'll all eat our fill and all act like fools!
And thank the Gods it's Yule!

Here's to Ingvi-Freyr the lord of the feast,
We'll soon be devouring your sweet roasted beast,
Your boar at your side, your ship in the dock,
And who could forget your massive great...

Bring me more meat and bring me more mead!
We'll tell tall tales and boast of our deeds!
We'll all eat our fill and all act like fools!
And thank the Gods it's Yule!

Here's to Ægir the greatest of hosts,
Without your sweet nectar there would be no toasts,
Your mead keeps on flowing, we're really in luck,
If we keep it up we'll be too drunk to...

Bring me more meat and bring me more mead!
We'll tell tall tales and boast of our deeds!
We'll all eat our fill and all act like fools!
And thank the Gods it's Yule!

Here's to Thor, your strength we can't test,
But why are you feasting wearing a dress?
There's Jotunns a-drooling admiring your frock,
But under your skirts there's only a...

Bring me more meat and bring me more mead!
We'll tell tall tales and boast of our deeds!
We'll all eat our fill and all act like fools!
And thank the Gods it's Yule!

Here's to Odin so great and so wise,
Huggin and Munnin your all seeing eyes,
Whilst Geri is sleeping, and Freki is mewing,
Your mind is not here, you'd rather be...

Bring me more meat and bring me more mead!
We'll tell tall tales and boast of our deeds!
We'll all eat our fill and all act like fools!
And thank the Gods it's Yule!

Here's to Loki the master of tricks,
So cunning and witty and sly and slick,
You know the flaws of all in their halls,
But wait what is that? A goat tied to your...

Bring me more meat and bring me more mead!
We'll tell tall tales and boast of our deeds!
We'll all eat our fill and all act like fools!
And thank the Gods it's Yule!

Hail the ancestors, hail the wights!
Hail the Gods and Godesses this night!
Hail to Yorkshire, 'cos Yorkshire is right,
'Cos if it's not Yorkshire it's shite!

Heathens o' Yorkshire

Who's tha a'hailin all t' Gods?
Heathens o' Yorkshire.
Who's tha a'hailin all t' Gods?
Who's tha a'hailin all t' Gods?
Heathens o' Yorkshire,
Heathens o' Yorkshire,
Heathens o' Yorkshire.

Tha's been a'drinkin all o't' mead,
Heathens o' Yorkshire.
Tha's been a'drinkin all o't' mead,
Tha's been a'drinkin all o't' mead,
Heathens o' Yorkshire,
Heathens o' Yorkshire,
Heathens o' Yorkshire.

Tha's bahn t' die o' too much mead,
Heathens o' Yorkshire.
Tha's bahn t' die o' too much mead,
Tha's bahn t' die o' too much mead,
Heathens o' Yorkshire,
Heathens o' Yorkshire,
Heathens o' Yorkshire.

Then t'Valhalla we'll send thee,
Heathens o' Yorkshire,
Then t'Valhalla we'll send thee,
Then t'Valhalla we'll send thee,
Heathens o' Yorkshire,
Heathens o' Yorkshire,
Heathens o' Yorkshire.

Nidhog'll come an` eyt thee up,
Heathens o' Yorkshire,
Nidhog'll come an` eyt thee up,
Nidhog'll come an` eyt thee up,
Heathens o' Yorkshire,

Heathens o' Yorkshire,
Heathens o' Yorkshire.

Ravens'll come an' peck tha eyes,
Heathens o' Yorkshire,
Ravens'll come an' peck tha eyes,
Ravens'll come an' peck tha eyes,
Heathens o' Yorkshire,
Heathens o' Yorkshire,
Heathens o' Yorkshire.

Then us'll 'eyt a funeral feast,
Heathens o' Yorkshire,
Then us'll 'eyt a funeral feast,
Then us'll 'eyt a funeral feast,
Heathens o' Yorkshire,
Heathens o' Yorkshire,
Heathens o' Yorkshire.

Then us'll drink up all o't' mead,
Heathens o' Yorkshire,
Then us'll drink up all o't' mead,
Then us'll drink up all o't' mead,
Heathens o' Yorkshire,
Heathens o' Yorkshire,
Heathens o' Yorkshire.

That's wheear we end up back wid thee,
Heathens o' Yorkshire,
That's wheear we end up back wid thee,
That's wheear we end up back wid thee,
Heathens o' Yorkshire,
Heathens o' Yorkshire,
Heathens o' Yorkshire!

Viking Soul
-Alda Björk Ólafsdóttir

Being a Viking you're meant to be strong,
And that I am don't get me wrong,
But I got a heart that melts easily,
And my eyes seem to leak too frequently.

The Norns seem to have weaved it for me,
That I should be tested too frequently,
Maybe they know that I can take it,
Maybe I know how to fake it.

Viking Soul,
That I am.
Viking Soul,
That I am.

Yes I get tired and want to lay down,
Lie by the waterfall with its only sound,
Hug mother nature, yes I hugged a tree,
Actually it was mother nature who hugged me.

So life goes on and with a smile,
I fight through the battlefield wounded but alive,
When I'm knocked down, I rise up again,
Stronger and meaner this is not the end.

Viking Soul,
That I am,
Viking Soul,
That I am.

The Tears of the Wolf
– In Loving Memory of Yellowstone Wolf 926

- Alda Björk Ólafsdóttir

Wolf 926, survivor, alpha, fighter,
She's a mother and partner to wolf 925.
Her puppies are growing and new ones on the way,
She tricks the biggest cow into becoming her pray.

They feast and soak up the sun but hurry they must,
As they had wondered too far to the wrong side of their track,
But it was too late as their rival pack had already come,
Wolf 925 stands his ground with her puppies 926 must run.

Run, run, run away,
Úfasöngur verður úlfagrátur,
Run, run, run away.

Wolf 925 is dead but his family he saved,
Now a single mother wolf 926 struggles are hard,
Survival is doubtful no matter how brave,
Another day another battle, hiding in her cave.

Suddenly deep within her den there is present danger,
The killer alpha had found her and she stood no chance,
Kill is what he´s there for but she has other plans,
Quickly composes herself and turns on her charm.

She didn't Run, run, run away,
Úfasöngur verður úlfagrátur,
Run, run, run away.

The big papa Alpha male is taken by surprise,
She shows no fear, she´s strong and she is wise,
Her trickery works and her puppies are now safe,
A new protector of her family, her courage saved the day.

But as the new pack family settle in their nest,
Their biggest enemy waits patiently with shotgun resting on his chest.
As he gets aim through is sight he tightens his grip,
Then pulls the triggers and wolf 926 is hit.

She should have run, run, run away,
Úfasöngur verður úlfagrátur,
Should have run, run, run away.

It's too late to run, run, run away,
Úfasöngur verður úlfagrátur,
Too late to run, run, run away.

She howls and her cries can be heard for thousands of miles,
Slowly she falls as the blood pours from her veins,
As she falls dead you can hear Thor's anger with thunder,
She lost to the cruelest of all animals,
The human hunter.

Cries of the Heart
-Alda Björk Ólafsdóttir

As he´s looking over his once beautiful highlands,
Once filled with love now savaged by violence,
The chieftain's only daughter as sweet as she could be,
He was set to marry but he knew, she is not for me.

As they both had loved another neither wanted to stay,
Then a striking Viking came and whisked her away,
Now he was free to love the only girl he ever loved,
A simple farmer's daughter from the Nordic of folks.

Souls ripped apart,
Even strong men they cry,
As their true love is sacrificed,
When their loved ones they die,
Vikings versus Celts,
In the cries of the hearts.

But as a man makes his plans the Norns might not agree,
Your path has been woven for you, you cannot foresee,
The chieftain he is furious his wishes have been ignored,
Revenge will soon come knocking, now death was at their door.

May all the Norsemen and their daughters die before I rest,
The highlands became a bloody bath as he carried out his quest,
Now a sad and lonely figure the highlander reflects,
Wondering if the chieftain's daughter and her Viking man was a success.

Souls ripped apart,
Even strong men they cry,
As their true love is sacrificed,
When their loved ones they die,
Vikings versus Celts,
In the cries of the hearts.

Heathens of Yorkshire

All this pain,
On these plains,
For the souls I weep,
As I fall asleep.

Souls ripped apart,
Even strong men they cry,
As their true love is sacrificed,
When their loved ones they die,
Vikings versus Celts,
In the cries of the hearts.

Gifts of the Goddesses
-Adrian Spendlow

Blessing the Goddesses; Blessing the Earth,
Experience again your Viking rebirth.
Battle for love; believe in Freyja,
Dive naked through waterfalls, Brinhild is here.
As Amma will harvest and all will grow,
So Lin will serve; all beauty to show.
Be old yet young be gathered by Berchta,
Gently remember who you are through Snotra.
Let Lofn be stirring your belief in romance,
Be not forbidden, feel Sjofn's advance.
Syn will defend you: Gefion make pure,
Sunlight dances on water for the eyes of Saga.
Birth be powerful; be proudful as Rind,
Fly high with Sun; dance on the wind.
Gna washes us clean; Audumla feeds,
Fulla will fill, bringing forth all your needs.
Jorð is at one with you, ever aware,
Skuld, Urd, Verdani: your self is laid bare.
Sif brings us gold; the sun on the corn,
Nanna's womanly peace gives joy reborn.
Nurture regardless Angraboda,
Be the mother of Gods; be as Bestla.
Stronger than Thor, learn Glima with Elli,
The power of Eir for healing and mercy.
Nerthus has berthed us be at one in the world,
Be guarded Sinmorano no wounding unfurled.
As mighty as Thrud you are Thorsdottir,
Rule your own soul, the power of Skirnir.
Var fills our heart to make oaths of love,
For Vor nothing is hidden within or above.
Gleam with a beauty for Menglad will heal,

Rise again with Gulveig to truly feel.
Nine Mothers rise over us, take us away,
Feel as strongly as Ran does; be free to say.
Walk the plains with Ida you animal spirit,
Be mother as Mothir as moments befit.
Sygin forever brings freedom from pain,
View the future with Groa; tomorrow is plain.
These are the Goddesses bringing rebirth,
Fjorgyn's children – Mother Earth.
These are the Goddesses bringing rebirth,
Fjorgyn's children – Mother Earth.

Rituals

A Blót to Thor

This blót to Thor can be used as it is, to honour the thunderer. It can also be used as a template for creating your own blóts to any of the Gods or Goddesses you wish, by substituting other prayers from the book, or your own words.

This ritual can be done by yourself or in a group. It can be done inside or outside, but it is recommended that it is done somewhere quiet, where the ritual will not be disturbed. These days it is also well worth reminding the participants to switch off their phones and devices.

How you set up for the ritual is up to you. At Heathens of Yorkshire we set up an altar to the north of the participants. The Goði, or person leading the ritual stands by the altar, with the other participants facing the altar. How you stand will depend on your groups preferences, and the practicality of the space.

The altar itself can be as simple or elaborate as you like. As a minimum it should have a representation of the deity that is being honoured, and a bowl to receive liquid offerings. We use mead in our rituals, but you can use whatever feels right to you.

Use these words to begin the ritual:

There were once but two realms, separated by a great, inconceivable void. The endless, baron chasm called Ginnungagap. To one side lay the icy, frozen land of Niflheim, too cold for any creature to survive. On the other, Muspelheim lay, where the raging fires prevented even the hardiest life. When these forces finally met, so the first being was created, the first of the mighty giants, Ymir.

Nurtured by the great cow, Audhumla, Ymir spawned the race of giants. Audhumla licked at the ice for her own sustenance, and slowly but surely released Buri, first of the Æsir, from his frozen prison. Buri bore a son, Bor, who, with the giantess Bestla, bore three sons, Odin, Vili and Ve.

The three brothers grew, and once they were strong enough, rose up and slew the great Ymir, and with his corpse created a home. That home, is our home, where we are born, where we will die, where we will see great joy, where we will suffer terrible hardship, and where we will witness every emotion. From Ymir's skull, they created the sky above us, from his brains came the clouds, which give us the rains. His muscles formed the land on which we live, and the blood that poured from his wounds that day was to become the great oceans.

Having made our home, they made us. From a trunk of ash, and a trunk of elm, they made Ask and Embla, the first of our human ancestors. Their descendants would later mate with Rígr, to make us who we are today, not just creations of the Gods, but distant relatives. Here we stand, as our ancestors stood, the product of the Gods, in the home the Gods fought to create for us. Here we stand, as our descendants will stand, to honour the Gods, wights and ancestors, until the chaos returns, and the realms of Gods and men fall.

Hold up the mead and speak these words:

Bragi, bless this brew, we are grateful for this, the gift of Ægir.

Distribute the mead to the participants.

We call upon the Æsir, we call upon the Vanir. We call upon the wights and the ancestors. We ask you to join us for this blót in honour of Thor.

Pour an offering of mead for the deities.

Hail to mighty Thor!
Friend to all sons and daughters of the earth,
Foe to the children of Þorn.
Mjölnir's wielder,
Your winds guide the shield provider of the warships prow;
Your rains bring life to the field;
Your high flames light the sky.
Serpent's bane,
You empty more ale-prows than all the kin of Ingvi-Freyr;
You travel far with the wolf's father;
You protect the realms of Gods and men.
Thunderer! Warder! Protector!
We call to you!
Hail Thor!

Pour an offering of mead for Thor.

Hail to Thor!
Hammer-wielder! Lightening-Rider!
Hail to he who brings us strength and courage on the lonely roads of life.
May you inspire us to be courageous, to be brave and strong!
May we think of you every time the thunder rolls or lightning flashes across the stormy sky!
May we smile at storm-time for we know you are with us Thor!
When red sky's smile let us know it is your red beard blown by the winds!
Hail to you Thor, smasher of giants!
Hail to you Thor, strongest of Gods!
And may you forever protect us!

Pour an offering of mead for Thor.

Hail to the companions of Thor!
As the mighty thunderer rides across the sky,
Fiery in both look and temperament,
Protecting Gods and men from the chaos,
We remember you, his companions.
We thank you for the support you give him,
So that he can continue to protect us.
We thank the goats, Snarler and Grinder,
For pulling the loud riders chariot,
And providing him with sustenance.
We thank Þjálfi and Röskva,
For your dedication to serving your master.
We thank Thor's travelling companion,
The trickster, whose devious skills compliment Asa-Thor's strength,
And help him to overcome his foes.
We thank Sif, his bride, and Jarnsaxa, mother of his children,
And we honour Mjölnir, hammer of the Gods,
The mighty weapon with which the hallower protects us.
Hail the companions of Thor!

Pour an offering of mead for the companions of Thor.

At this point you can conduct a one round sumbel, where all participants can make any offerings, and speak any additional words that they wish in honour of Thor.

Close the ritual with the words:

Words have been spoken,
Offerings have been made,
From the Gods, to the earth, to us,
From us, to the earth, to the Gods,
A gift for a gift,
Hail!

Midsummer Blót to Sunna

Midsummer is an excellent time to gather with friends and family, to enjoy the good weather and give thanks to Sunna for her life giving warmth. A barbeque is a great way to hold a summer feast. Traditionally people would jump over fires for good luck, the fire being made from the remains of their midwinter greenery.

This simple blót to Sunna can be used at your gathering in her honour. All you need for the ritual is an offering of mead or other liquid. Begin the ritual as follows:

Friends! We are gathered here together to enjoy the good weather, long days, and each other's company. At this time of year we also give thanks to Sunna, the Goddess who drags the sun across the sky each day, with her chariot drawn by her horses Arvakr and Alsviðr.

To begin this ritual let us all close our eyes, turn our faces to the sun, and chant the rune Sowelu, the rune of the sun, to hallow this space, and prepare ourselves to worship Sunna.

Allow the chanting to continue for as long as seems natural, once the chanting has died out, hold up the mead and say:

Bragi, bless this brew, we are grateful for this, the gift of Ægir.

We call upon the Æsir and the Vanir, we call upon the wights and the ancestors! We ask you to join us this midsummer, for a blót to Sunna. Hail!

Pour an offering of mead.

Hail to Sunna!
Lady of light, lady of life!
Without your warming rays there would be nothing but darkness.
No life, no laughter, no love.
On long summer days we bask in your warm embrace,
On cold winter's afternoons we take comfort,
As we glimpse your face through the clouds.

Mani's sister, ever glowing day star,
May Arvakr and Alsviðr keep you ahead of the wolf.
Hail Sunna!

Pour an offering for Sunna. Then conduct a sumbel for people to speak any words they wish in honour of Sunna. After the sumbel, complete the ritual with these words:

Words have been spoken,
Offerings have been made.
From the Gods, to the earth, to us,
From us, to the earth, to the Gods.
A gift for a gift,
Hail!

Harvest Blót

Harvest was an important time for our ancestors; gathering the year's crops ready for the long winter ahead. These days many of us take our food for granted, now that it arrives nicely packaged, and we don't have to toil the field ourselves to get it. However it is just as important to thank the Gods for our food now as it ever was. This ritual should be held at the time of the harvest to give thanks. For the ritual you will need a simple alter to the Gods and offerings. These offerings will ideally be local produce. Begin the ritual as follows:

We gather together here today to thank the Gods for our bountiful harvest. Whilst we may not have grown the crops, or raised the animals ourselves, we are just as dependant on the Gods granting us food as we ever were.

Raise the mead and say:

Bragi, bless this brew, we are grateful for this, the gift of Ægir.

Thor, who's chariot crosses the sky, bringing the gentle rains that nurture the crops, we ask you to hallow and protect this sacred space. Hail Thor!

Pour an offering of mead for Thor.

Hail to the lord of the harvest!
As the frosts melted, we asked you to fertilise our crops,
To guard the seeds as they germinated and sprouted,
To nourish the shoots with gentle rains,
And protect them as they grew.
All this you have done,
And for that we that we give thanks this day.
The time has come to harvest this crop,
The product of our shared efforts,
So that we may be sustained through the long winter.
This crop is your gift to us, and so we share it with you,
And we honour you, oh Freyr,

As we take in this crop with glad hearts.
Hail Freyr!

Pour an offering of mead for Freyr.

We call to the wights of the land!
You have shared your space with us,
Allowed us to grow our crops,
And raise our animals,
In peace and prosperity.
For this, we give you thanks.
Hail the wights!

Pour an offering of mead for the wights.

We call to the Vanir!
All those Gods and Goddesses who nurture the earth.
Njörð, elder Van, who shares with us the bounty of the sea,
Your twin children, Freyr and Freyja,
And all the rest of your kin.
We thank you for sharing this harvest with us,
And we in turn share it with you.
Hail the Vanir!

Pour an offering of mead for the Vanir.

Place the offerings you wish to give in thanks for the harvest upon the altar.

Words have been spoken,
Offerings have been made,
From the Gods, to the earth to us,
From us, to the earth to the Gods.
A gift for a gift,
Hail!

After the blót, hold a feast of local produce, and toast the Gods as your enjoy their bounty. If you do happen to grow your own crops, follow the tradition of leaving the last ear of corn in the field for Sleipnir. This could be done with any crops you grow.

Heathen Remembrance Service

This version of the traditional Remembrance Service has been adapted for use by heathens to mark Remembrance Sunday/Armistice Day. Starting at 1050 should mean that the 2 minutes silence is held at 1100.

Welcome to all gathered here, on Remembrance Sunday, to honour the fallen, and all those who have made personal sacrifice in the service of their country.

We call upon the wights of land, air and water. We ask you to join us here this day. Hail the wights!

We call upon the ancestors, to whom we owe everything that we are, and without whom we would not be. We ask you to join us here this day. Hail the ancestors!

We call upon the Gods; Æsir and Vanir. Mighty ones, shining ones, high ones. We ask you to join us here this day. Hail the Gods!

Freyja, warrior Goddess and first chooser of the slain, for whom you weep golden tears of compassion. We give you thanks for welcoming our glorious dead to Folkvangr. Queen of Valkyries, Goddess of love, lady of magic, we honour you. Hail Freyja!

Odin, Lord of War, leader of the Einherjar, master of Valhalla, we call to you! Wise one, who's Valkyries choose those who will fight alongside you at Ragnarok. You who knows sacrifice, and is not afraid to do that which may seem wrong in order to achieve the ultimate goal, we honour you. Hail Odin!

Ran, beautiful Lady of the deep, we thank you for hosting all those sailors lost at sea, in your great hall beneath the waves. Hail Ran!

We gather here to honour the fallen. Those brave warriors who have made the ultimate sacrifice in defence our of nation and our people, and who will do battle again, when the Gjallarhorn sounds. We honour too those who have returned, witnesses of the true horrors of war, to be once more amongst the people they protect. We remember too all the civilian casualties of all conflicts across the globe, and we honour those who are serving now, at this very moment risking their lives on sea, land and air, so that we may sleep safely in peace and frith.

Reading – The Rainbow, Sgt Leslie Coulson, killed on the Western Front in 1916

Watch the white dawn gleam,
To the thunder of hidden guns.
I hear the hot shells scream
Through skies as sweet as a dream
Where the silver dawn-break runs.
And stabbing of light
Scorches the virginal white.
But I feel in my being the old, high, sanctified thrill,
And I thank the gods that the dawn is beautiful still.

From death that hurtles by
I crouch in the trench day-long,
But up to a cloudless sky
From the ground where our dead men lie
A brown lark soars in song.
Through the tortured air,
Rent by the shrapnel's flare,
Over the troubleless dead he carols his fill,
And I thank the gods that the birds are beautiful still.

Where the parapet is low
And level with the eye
Poppies and cornflowers glow
And the corn sways to and fro
In a pattern against the sky.
The gold stalks hide
Bodies of men who died
Charging at dawn through the dew to be killed or to kill.
I thank the gods that the flowers are beautiful still.

When night falls dark we creep
In silence to our dead.
We dig a few feet deep
And leave them there to sleep -
But blood at night is red,
Yea, even at night,
And a dead man's face is white.
And I dry my hands, that are also trained to kill,
And I look at the stars - for the stars are beautiful still.

Airforce Prayer

Mighty Thor!
Who tears through the clouds in your chariot,
And with Mjölnir brings the storm,
Look with favour upon the Royal Air Force.
Make us a tower of strength to our Queen and to our country.
Help us to do our duty with prudence and with fearlessness,
Confident that in life or in death we will protect our kin.
Grant this in the name of the Gods.
Hail!

A Soldier's Prayer

I am going to war,
Leaving loved ones behind.
I am leaving what is precious,
But I´m not going alone.
The Gods are with me,
In all the dark places.

Æsir, ease their hearts,
When my people miss me.
Æsir, stand with me,
When I am facing death.
Æsir, look after my loved ones,
As I would.

The Naval Prayer

Odin, Skyfather, lord of war, who rules over Asgard; Ægir, father of the waves; Rán, gracious host of those lost at sea; Njörð, who rules where the sea meets the shore; mighty Thor, master of tides until the wolf breaks his bonds, Hail! We honour you with word and deed, and ask you to bless the fleet in which we serve. Preserve us from the dangers of the sea, and grant us the strength to overcome the violence of the enemy; that we may be a safeguard unto our most gracious Sovereign Lady, Queen Elizabeth, and her dominions, and a security for such as pass on the seas upon their lawful occasions; that the inhabitants of our island may in frith honour our Gods; and that we may return victorious to enjoy the blessings of the land, with the fruits of our labours; and with a thankful remembrance of thy blessings to honour our Gods, wights and ancestors. Hail!

They shall grow not old, as we that are left grow old, Age shall not weary them nor the years condemn. At the going down of the sun, and in the morning We will remember them. *Response*: We will remember them.

(At 1100) Last Post. Lower standards.

2 Minutes silence.

Reveille. Raise standards.

Laying of wreaths.

When you go home,
Tell them of us and say,
For your tomorrow,
We gave our today.

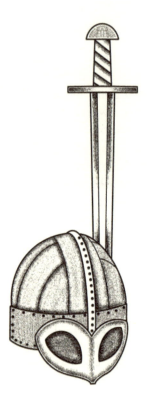

Mothers' Night Blót

Mothers' Night is held as part of the festival of Yule. Some celebrate it on the night before the winter solstice, others on the 24th of December. Regardless of when it is held, it is a night to remember all of our female ancestors. Before you begin, prepare a list of all of the female ancestors that you know of, so that their names can be read out. You may also want to prepare an altar with photographs and mementos of those you wish to honour.

Open the blót with these words:

Hail to red bearded Thor! Hallow and protect this sacred space.

Raise the mead and say:

Bragi, bless this brew, we are grateful for this, the gift of Ægir.

Distribute the mead to the participants.

We call upon the Æsir and the Vanir, we call upon the wights and the ancestors. We ask you to join us this Mothers' Night, for this blót to the Disir.

Pour an offering of mead for the deities.

Hail to the mother of mothers!
Hail to the Queen of Asgard!
Hail to Frigg!
We call to you this mother's night.
Caring one, kind one, loving one,
We thank you for guiding all mothers,
Giving them the strength to raise their children,
And support their families in the best way they can.
All of our mother line, going back to the beginning,
Watch over us, for we are their children.
Through your shining example they nurture us,
And help us to raise our own children,
So that our families may live forever.
Hail Frigg, mother of us all!

Pour an offering of mead for Frigg.

Hail to the Disir!
Ancient women, grandmothers, mothers.
You brought life to our ancestors, and to us.
You raised us, either in your own life time,
or through your spiritual guidance.

You helped us grow, to become who we are today.
Now we are grown, you continue to help us,
In all matters of the family.
Through your strength you guide us,
Helping us to raise future generations.
We thank you for the gift of life,
For without you we could not be.
Hail the Disir!

Pour an offering of mead for the Disir.

Read out the names of the Disir to be remembered.

Hold a one round sumbel where participants can make any offerings, and speak any words they wish to in honour of the Disir.

Close the blót with these words:

Words have been spoken, offerings have been made,
from the Gods, to the earth to us,
from us to the earth to the Gods, a gift for a gift.

Yule Blót to Odin

Yule is a time when we give thanks for the year that has passed, and look ahead to the year to come. It is also a time when the wild hunt rides across the sky. This blót honours the Alfather. It also gives the chance for those participating to take a rune to guide them in the year to come. For that reason you will need at least one set of runes. The runes should be in a bag or container, so that they can be selected without seeing them.

Open the blót with these words:

There were once but two realms, separated by a great, inconceivable void. The endless, baron chasm called Ginnungagap. To one side lay the icy, frozen land of Niflheim, too cold for any creature to survive. On the other, Muspelheim lay, where the raging fires prevented even the hardiest life. When these forces finally met, so the first being was created, the first of the mighty giants, Ymir.

Nurtured by the great cow, Audhumla, Ymir spawned the race of giants. Audhumla licked at the ice for her own sustenance, and slowly but surely released Buri, first of the Æsir, from his frozen prison. Buri bore a son, Bor, who, with the giantess Bestla, bore three sons, Odin, Vili and Ve.

The three brothers grew, and once they were strong enough, rose up and slew the great Ymir, and with his corpse created a home. That home, is our home, where we are born, where we will die, where we will see great joy, where we will suffer terrible hardship, and where we will witness every emotion. From Ymir's skull, they created the sky above us, from his brains came the clouds, which give us the rains. His muscles formed the land on which we live, and the blood that poured from his wounds that day was to become the great oceans.

Having made our home, they made us. From a trunk of ash, and a trunk of elm, they made Ask and Embla, the first of our human ancestors. Their descendants would later mate with Rígr, to make us who we are today, not just creations of the Gods, but distant relatives. Here we stand, as our ancestors stood, the product of the Gods, in the home the Gods fought to create for us. Here we stand, as our descendants will stand, to honour the Gods, wights and ancestors, until the chaos returns, and the realms of Gods and men fall.

Raise the mead and say:

Bragi, bless this brew, we are grateful for this, the gift of Ægir.

Distribute the mead.

Æsir, Vanir, wights and ancestors, we call to you this yuletide, we ask you to join us in the blót to the Alfather.

Pour an offering of mead for the deities.

To the lord of the long night hail!
Sleipnir's rider, you tear across the sky, with the hunt in tow,
Bringing death to the old year, making way for the life of the new.
This Yule night we thank you for the gift of the runes,
The knowledge that you sacrificed so much for,
Hanging for nine days from the windy tree.
God of madness, we honour you as we gather with our family,
On this longest and darkest of nights.
Hail Odin!

Pour an offering of mead for Odin.

Odin, you gave us the gift of the runes. We take up those very runes now, as we seek an insight into what the year ahead holds for us.

Each person reaches into the bag in turn, and takes one rune, that will guide them for the year ahead. After the blót, they can choose to share their rune with others, or keep it to themselves. Those with greater knowledge of the runes can help those with less experience to interpret what the rune could be telling them.

Once the runes are selected, hold a one round sumbel where those gathered can make any offerings, and speak any words they wish to in honour of Odin.

Close the blót with these words:

Words have been spoken,
offerings have been made,
From the Gods, to the earth, to us,
From us, to the earth, to the Gods,
A gift for a gift,
Hail!

Naming Ceremony

The first ritual of anyone's life who is born into a heathen family is likely to be their naming ceremony. This is a joyous time of celebration, to be shared with close family and friends, both those who are still with us, and those who have moved on. Whereas most rituals are often best carried out outside in nature, the naming ceremony is one ritual that is best carried out in the family home, so that it can be shared with the house spirits and ancestors.

As this is an important life ritual, it is important to be fully prepared for it. This could include a special outfit for the person being named, gifts for them from those attending, and a feast to be held in their honour. You will also need a liquid offering, traditionally mead, as this will be used to bless the child.

The ritual should be lead by one parent (traditionally the child's father, but this can be adapted to suit your family), with the other parent (traditionally the child's mother) entering the room and presenting the child. At the start of the ritual, everyone except the parent presenting the child should gather in the room that is considered the heart of the home, with the parent and child waiting outside of the door.

The parent leading the ritual should start the ritual with these words:

Red bearded Thor! Hallow and protect this space, in which we gather to welcome the child of [father] and [mother].

Hold up the mead and say:

Bragi, bless this brew, we are grateful for this, the gift of Ægir.

We call upon the Æsir, we call upon the Vanir, we call upon the house wights and the wights of this land, we call upon the ancestors of the [mother's] and [father's] families. We ask you to join us for this naming ritual.

The parent presenting the child should knock 9 times on the door, and then enter the room with the child. They should walk straight to the parent leading the ritual, hold the child towards them and say:

I present to you your [son/daughter/child]. I hereby give them the first and greatest of today's gifts, as I name them [child's name]. I do this before our friends and family, before the wights and before the Gods.

They then pass the child to the parent leading the ritual, who takes the child and says:

Welcome [child's name] to our family and to our community. I present you to our friends and family, I present you to the wights, and to the Gods.

Thor, warder, I ask you to protect this child, that they may serve both our family and our community.

Dip a finger in the mead, and mark the sign of the hammer on the child's forehead.

We call to the ancestors. We ask you to accept [child's name] into our family and our community. We will tell them your stories and teach them of your lives, that they may keep your memories alive. In exchange we ask that you watch over them, and pass on your wisdom to them, that they may become the best person they can be. Hail the ancestors!

Pour an offering for the ancestors.

We call to the house spirits. We ask you to accept [child's name] into your home. We will teach them to respect your space, and in return we ask that you treat them with the same warmth you treat us. Hail the house spirits!

Pour an offering for the house spirits.

We call to the Æsir and the Vanir. We present [child's name] to you. We shall tell them of your deeds, and teach them to honour you. We hope that their deeds shall please you, or at least entertain you! Hail the Gods and Goddesses!

Pour an offering for the Gods and Goddesses.

Those in attendance now take it in turns to approach the child, starting with the parents, then the family, and then the friends. Each person presents any gifts they may have for the child, speaks any words they wish, and where appropriate may swear an oath to the child. If you have nominated one or more person to be responsible for the child's spiritual upbringing, they may choose to swear the following oath to the child:

I, [name] hereby swear in front of the Gods, wights and ancestors, and those gathered here today, to guide you, [child's name], in your spiritual journey. I swear to help your parents to teach you the stories of the Gods, and how to live your life as an honourable member of our community.

Once everyone has taken their turn, speak the following words to end the ritual:

Words have been spoken, offerings have been made.
From the Gods, to the earth, to us,
From us, to the earth, to the Gods.
A gift for a gift,
Hail!

Home Blessing Ritual

Moving into a new home is an important time in anyone's life. This new place will be where you spend a significant amount of your time. A place where you should feel safe and at ease. It is also important to remember that you are not alone in this space. The dwelling is likely to already be home to one or more spirits, or housewights. Building a positive relationship with these spirits is essential. You must respect them, and gain their respect. Sharing your home with an ill willing wight is not a pleasant experience!

This ritual is designed to make a good first impression with the wights, but it is important that you continue to honour and respect them throughout your time in the home. It is particularly important to remember them whenever you are baking or brewing, to ensure they help, rather than hinder the process.

For this ritual you will need an offering of flowers for the house wights, and mead for the Gods and ancestors.

To begin the ritual, all those who are moving into the home, and any guest they have invited to the ritual should gather at the front of the home. The head of the household, or a nominated person, should lead the participants in a procession around the full perimeter of the home (or as far around it as is practical) back to the front door. During the procession, the participant should chant the rune 'othela', the rune of the home. On returning to the front door, mark the othela rune on or near the door. This could be done in chalk, or simply in mead.

Stand facing the door and say:

Thor! Thunderer, warder, hallow and protect our family home.

Open the door. Take a moment to look inside before crossing the threshold, then cross it, speaking these words as you do:

Wights of this place! Our family comes to your home. We come with good intentions, to share this space with you, not to drive you from it. We bring you offerings, and we bring you good will. Hail to the wights of this place!

Proceed to the room at the heart of the home, this could be the living room, dining room or kitchen. Place an offering of flowers for the house wights. Afterwards speak these words:

We call to the Æsir, we call to the Vanir! Great Gods and Goddesses, we invite you into our new home. For as long as we inhabit this place, you will always be welcome here, you will always be honoured here. Hail the Æsir! Hail the Vanir!

Pour an offering of mead.

We call to the ancestors! Those who watch over us, who guide us. We invite you into our new home. For as long as we inhabit this place, you will always be welcome here, you will always be honoured here. Hail the ancestors!

You can now conduct a sumbel for anyone to add any words, and give an offerings they wish. On completion, finish the ritual with these words:

Words have been spoken,
Offerings have been made.
From the Gods to the earth to us,
From us to the earth to the Gods.
A gift for a gift,
Hail!

Wedding Ceremony

For most people their wedding day is one of the most important days of their lives. It is therefore very important that it is properly prepared for. The bare minimum required for the ceremony I have described here are an officiant, the couple to be married, an oath ring, and rings for the couple to exchange. If the couple are part of a kindred, the oath ring used should be the oath ring of the kindred. If this is not an option a family oath ring could be used, or an oath ring made or purchased especially for the occasion. The couple may choose to wed in traditional dress, or in modern clothing.

In England, at the time of writing, heathen ceremonies are not legally recognised, and so a separate legal ceremony will need to take place. The laws are different in different countries. If you are lucky enough to live in a country where heathen wedding ceremonies are legally recognised, you will not need a separate civil ceremony.

Almost every element of this ceremony can be changed and adapted to suit the couples needs; this is purely an example of how a ceremony could be conducted. I have used the terms 'bride' and 'groom' throughout, but there is no reason why this ceremony could not be used for a same-sex couple. The ceremony contains a mixture of traditional elements, and elements from the modern wedding ceremony.

The physical layout of the ceremony is up to you, but if it is taking place indoors, you should have an area to place offerings and/or a bowl for liquid offerings.

As the ceremony begins the official should stand by the altar, or central area with the groom, who should be accompanied by a trusted friend or group of friends. The bride should walk to meet the groom, accompanied by a family member (traditionally the father). This marks the start of the ceremony, and can be accompanied by music.

The officiant then speaks these words:

Welcome one and all. We are gathered here today before the Gods to join [bride] and [groom] in marriage. We call upon the Æsir, we call upon the Vanir. We call upon the wights and the ancestors. We ask you to join us, and witness the marriage between [bride] and [groom].

Pour an offering.

Thor! Thunderer! Hallow and protect this sacred space.

If the couple wish, you can now have a reading from the lore of their choosing. This could be a passage from the Havamal, the Eddas or any other reading the couple feel is significant to them. If the couple have any Gods or Goddesses that are particularly important to them, they may wish for prayers to those deities to be included here. After the reading, the officiant should hold up the oath ring and invoke Var:

Hail to Var!
Honest Goddess, witness the oaths we swear here today.
Truthful Goddess, bless all those who keep their word.
Honourable Goddess, bring vengeance upon the untrustworthy.
Var, you listen carefully to all oaths spoken,
Remembering the details, ensuring they are upheld.
Friend to those who stand firmly by their pledge,
Punisher of the liar and the double crosser,
You guide us in upholding our honourable reputations.
Hail Var!

Pour an offering for Var.

The bride and groom will now swear oaths to one another, to seal their bonds, and recognise each other as their sworn partner.

Ideally the oaths will be written by the couple themselves, but the following words can be used. Oaths are extremely important in heathenry, and it is important not to swear anything you cannot keep. For this reason 'til death do us part' is much less likely to feature in a heathen wedding oath, as whilst the end of a marriage is not something most people want to think about at it's beginning, oaths are binding, and so a line such as 'for as long as our love shall last' gives the couple options in the future.

As the oaths are sworn, both partners should hold the oath ring, and look at each other as the words are spoken.

Groom: I [name] hereby swear to you [bride's name] in the presence of the Gods, the wights, the ancestors, and those gathered here today, to love you, to protect you, to be loyal to you, and to serve you as an equal partner, in joy and in sorrow, in sickness and in health, for as long as our love shall last.

Bride: I [name] hereby swear to you [groom's name] in the presence of the Gods, the wights, the ancestors, and those gathered here today, to love you, to protect you, to be loyal to you, and to serve you as an equal partner, in joy and in sorrow, in sickness and in health, for as long as our love shall last.

The officiant now takes the rings, hold them up and says:

The oaths have been sworn upon an oath ring. The oaths shall be forever bound in that oath ring. These rings, which the couple shall wear, not only act as a visible sign of their marriage, but also as a reminder to them of the oaths they have sworn this day.

The officiant hands the rings to the couple for them to exchange. On completion, the officiant should speak these words:

[Name] and [name] have sworn oaths to each other, they have exchanged rings to symbolise these oaths. In the presence of the Gods, the wights, the ancestors, and those of you gathered here today, I pronounce them man and wife. You may now kiss the bride.

On completion of the ceremony a feast should be held in the couples honour. As the couple leave for this feast, it is traditional for them to be accompanied by a 'guard of honour' made up of trusted friends. If the couple wish to have children, it is traditional for Mjölnir to be laid in the brides lap at the feast, to symbolically ask Thor to bless them with fertility. The feast may also include all the usual elements of a modern wedding reception such as speeches, a first dance, and cake cutting.

Funeral

A funeral is a challenging time for any family. If the deceased was a heathen, it is likely they will want a heathen funeral. It is also likely that many of the friends and family who wish to pay their respects will not follow a heathen path, and may not know much about it. This funeral service aims to both give the departed the heathen service they would want, without excluding their non-heathen kin.

I have given three different options for the service depending on whether the departed died at sea, in battle, or in any other circumstances. The basic ceremony is the same for all three, the only difference being which deities are focused on, depending on where the departed is likely to spend their afterlife.

The layout of the service will depend on where it is taking place, for example at a crematorium or cemetery. This service can be used in any setting.

We gather here today to celebrate the life of [name], and pay our respects as they begin their journey from this world to the next. As many of you will know, in life [name] followed a heathen path, dedicated to the ancestors, the spirits of the land and the sea, and the old Gods. This service will honour their heathen beliefs.

We call upon the Æsir, we call upon the Vanir, we call upon the wights and the ancestors of the [surname] family. We ask you to join us here today as we say farewell to our beloved and departed kinsman/kinswoman/kinsperson.

We call to the ancestors.
Those who have come before us,
Who continue to guide us to become the best we can be.
Whether as warriors, as farmers, as mothers,
Whatever your trade, your deeds,
You not only provide us with an example,
But you continue to actively guide us in our lives,
Watching over your descendants as your own children.
We are the product of your loves and your lives,
And we shall do our utmost to uphold your honour and reputations.
Hail the ancestors!

If the deceased has died at sea, use the following invocation to Rán:

We call to the great hostess of the deep.
A kinsman has left us, and come to your door,
Seeking your protecting, your hospitality, and a seat in your hall.
They have walked the roads of men for the last time,
They have set sail, never to return to our hearth,
But instead to be with all those sailors,
Whose threads where cut amongst the roiling waves,
And found themselves at your mercy.
We make offering to you this day,
As they made offerings to you,
And ask that you take in our beloved kin,
Our seafarer, who knew your road well.
Born of a land they left behind,
Loved by a kin they sailed to protect.
In death they are with you,
For when they lived, they chose the sea.
Hail Rán!

If the deceased died in battle, use the following invocation to Odin and Freyja:

Odin, lord of Valhöll, Freyja, lady of Fölkvangr,
We call to you!
A warrior has left us, and joined your ranks.
There was a battle, here in Midgard,
The Valkyries came, and took our brave kinsman,
From our world to yours.
In life they fought to protect their family, their friends, their community.
Now they shall feast with you, fight with you, die beside you,
Each day, until the wolf breaks his bonds,
And they fight one final time,
On the field of Vígríðr.
May they serve you as faithfully as they have served us.
Hail Odin! Hail Freyja!

If the deceased has died of any other cause, use the following invocation to Hel:

Hail to the mistress of Helheim!
Loki's daughter, hostess of the dead,
We call to you.
A traveller approaches.
They are tired, they are weary,
Their feet are sore.
They have travelled for many miles and many days,
On a journey few look forward to making.
They have toiled, they have laughed,
They have loved, they have cried.
They have suffered, they have cared,
They have lived, they have died.
They have crossed the Gjöll bridge,
And now they stand before Éljúðnir,
Before you, seeking your hospitality.
Please grant them sanctuary,
That they might be reunited with their ancestors.
Amongst their loving kin,
That they might rest now,
Free of life's trials and tribulations.
With food, and drink, and company,
That one day we too shall join them,
To share stories by the hearth fire.
Hail Hel!

In heathenry we do not believe that the end of our lives on this earth is truly the end. We believe that our ancestors watch over us throughout our lives, guiding us, protecting us. [Name] is today joining those ancestors, in the next life. Whilst they are leaving us for now, they can look forward to a joyous reunion with those who have previously departed, and one day, when our time comes, we will see them again, and they shall welcome us, in another joyous reunion.

Now is the time for the eulogies. One or more person can speak about the departed, and their memories of them. They may also wish to recite poetry, a reading from the lore, or play music. Once this is complete, the officiant can conclude the service as follows:

[Name] has gone to be with their ancestors. In heathenry we believe that a person does not truly die so long as they are remembered. So long as we continue to tell their stories, drink toasts in their honour and keep them in a warm place in our hearts, they shall live on. Today is a celebration of [name's] life, as much as it is a day to grieve their passing. At the feast that will follow this service, you are encouraged to share stories, and remember our departed fondly. They too shall be feasting, in the halls beyond, sharing stories, telling jokes, and waiting for us to join them.

Cattle die and kinsmen die,
One day you too shall die.
But I know one thing that never dies,
And that is the fame we earn in life.

Cattle die and kinsmen die,
One day you too shall die.
But I know one thing that shall not die,
And that is the reputation of a good person.

About Heathens of Yorkshire

Heathens of Yorkshire is a local kith for heathens all over Yorkshire and the surrounding counties. It is an active group that meets at least monthly in different locations around the Gods' own county for ritual, discussion and socialising. The group also has a very active Facebook page where members can share information about heathenry.

The group is run by a kindred council who work hard to make sure the group provides the best possible experience for its members.

Heathens of Yorkshire is an inclusive group open to all those in the Yorkshire area who follow a heathen path regardless of race, sexuality, gender or disability. It is also open to their friends and family who want to find out more about the heathen way of life. If you would like to join the group, simple search for 'Heathens of Yorkshire' on Facebook or email kin@heathensofyorkshire.com.

Made in United States
Troutdale, OR
06/24/2023

10774148R00119